THE MAKING OF A PASTORAL PERSON

The Making of a Pastoral Person
Expanded and Revised Edition

REV. GERALD R. NIKLAS

ALBA·HOUSE house NEW·YORK

SOCIETY OF ST. PAUL, 2187 VICTORY BLVD., STATEN ISLAND, NEW YORK 10314

Library of Congress Cataloging-in-Publication Data

Niklas, Gerald R.
    The making of a pastoral person / Gerald R. Niklas. — Expanded
and rev. ed.
        p.   cm.
    ISBN 0-8189-0761-4
    1. Pastoral theology — Catholic Church. 2. Lay ministry — Catholic
Church. 3. Catholic Church — Clergy.   I. Title
BX1913.N57   1996
253'.07 — dc20   96-11427
                                                CIP

Produced and designed in the United States of America by the
Fathers and Brothers of the Society of St. Paul,
2187 Victory Boulevard, Staten Island, New York 10314,
as part of their communications apostolate.

ISBN: 0-8189-0761-4

Printing Information:

Current Printing - first digit   1   2   3   4   5   6   7   8   9   10

Year of Current Printing - first year shown

1996   1997   1998   1999   2000   2001

TABLE OF CONTENTS

PREFACE

WHEN ALBA HOUSE AGREED TO publish the first edition of this book in 1981, I was elated. I had begun writing on a high school newspaper and had taken several courses in writing in college, and now had several articles published. This prompted me to want to write a book. I dreamt of one day going into a bookstore and seeing my name on a book. Alba House helped to fulfill that dream, and I will always be grateful to them for this.

I was pleased over these years, at various national workshops and conventions, to be told by Clinical Pastoral Education supervisors that some of their students found the book to be of assistance to them. Some students especially found this or that chapter helpful. Other students found the book in general to assist them in their C.P.E. journey. I was happy that the book was helpful to others.

One C.P.E. supervisor noted wisely that *The Making of a Pastoral Person* gave insights into my C.P.E. journey. That's true. It also contained many of the thoughts of the supervisors and my peers during the journey.

When the first edition went out of print, some C.P.E. supervisors wrote asking me if I had any additional copies because some of their students wanted them. Eventually I wrote to Alba House asking about the possibility of republishing the book and possibly revising it. They were open to this suggestion and urged me to begin immediately revising, updating and enlarging the text. Chapters Eleven, Twelve and Thirteen are new to this edition.

As I read through the book, I noted that some parts were out of date, some of the language was sexist, and I did not now agree with some of the things that I had said. In addition, I needed to include more books authored by women, as well as more ideas about how certain events influenced women.

I am grateful for the continued growth that has occurred in me because of the students that I have had and the supervisors with whom I have interacted over the years. I am also grateful to the Consultation Committee at the Good Samaritan Hospital who have continued to gently challenge me to improve personally and to help the C.P.E. program continue to grow.

Finally I am grateful to the Catholic Health Association which has granted me permission to reproduce a number of my ideas in Chapter Eleven which previously appeared in the 1982 issue of *Health Progress*. A special thanks too goes to Bobette Good who diligently typed these pages for me.

Biblical Abbreviations

OLD TESTAMENT

Genesis	Gn	Nehemiah	Ne	Baruch	Ba
Exodus	Ex	Tobit	Tb	Ezekiel	Ezk
Leviticus	Lv	Judith	Jdt	Daniel	Dn
Numbers	Nb	Esther	Est	Hosea	Ho
Deuteronomy	Dt	1 Maccabees	1 M	Joel	Jl
Joshua	Jos	2 Maccabees	2 M	Amos	Am
Judges	Jg	Job	Jb	Obadiah	Ob
Ruth	Rt	Psalms	Ps	Jonah	Jon
1 Samuel	1 S	Proverbs	Pr	Micah	Mi
2 Samuel	2 S	Ecclesiastes	Ec	Nahum	Na
1 Kings	1 K	Song of Songs	Sg	Habakkuk	Hab
2 Kings	2 K	Wisdom	Ws	Zephaniah	Zp
1 Chronicles	1 Ch	Sirach	Si	Haggai	Hg
2 Chronicles	2 Ch	Isaiah	Is	Malachi	Ml
Ezra	Ezr	Jeremiah	Jr	Zechariah	Zc
		Lamentations	Lm		

NEW TESTAMENT

Matthew	Mt	Ephesians	Eph	Hebrews	Heb
Mark	Mk	Philippians	Ph	James	Jm
Luke	Lk	Colossians	Col	1 Peter	1 P
John	Jn	1 Thessalonians	1 Th	2 Peter	2 P
Acts	Ac	2 Thessalonians	2 Th	1 John	1 Jn
Romans	Rm	1 Timothy	1 Tm	2 John	2 Jn
1 Corinthians	1 Cor	2 Timothy	2 Tm	3 John	3 Jn
2 Corinthians	2 Cor	Titus	Tt	Jude	Jude
Galatians	Gal	Philemon	Phm	Revelation	Rv

THE MAKING OF A PASTORAL PERSON

CHAPTER ONE

PROCESS OF PASTORAL EDUCATION

I N MY OWN TRAINING FOR THE ministry I entered the seminary in September and for the most part never left it except for a two-week vacation at Christmas, a one-week vacation at Easter, and a three-month vacation in the summer. I never experienced any kind of co-op program where there was an attempt to integrate lofty theological principles and ideals with the "nitty gritty" of life. My preparation to meet the needs of people took place in isolation from people and their real problems. In contrast to that kind of training, I believe educating persons for any kind of ministry in the Church today needs to be based on relationships, experiences, reflection, and evaluation, emotionality, integration and decision making. As persons live in the world and interact with it, they relate to people, experience people and events, reflect and evaluate some of these experiences, emote because of these interactions, integrate some of them into their personalities, and make decisions in everyday living. Pastoral care education is a process, based on this understanding of life and assumes that these are necessary for true education. This process rightly assumes that these are necessary for true education. This process is assisted in supervised pastoral care programs such as those present in general hospitals, mental health centers, jails, churches, and other centers accredited by the United States Catholic Conference and/or the Association of Clinical Pastoral Education.[1]

Relationships

Supervisors relate to students as leaders, and this leadership is exercised in a manner in which there is a high degree of sharing responsibility and deciding together. Yet, it is assumed that education doesn't take place totally by consensus, but is assisted by some structure, e.g., a weekly schedule. Supervisors relate to students as persons with whom they are working together, rather than as persons who are working for them. Supervisors don't give their students all the "leg work" or unload their duties on the students, but relate to them more as colleagues than as superiors, as coaches more than lecturers. In this function as coaches, the leaders scrimmage with the supervisors at times in the daily work of pastoral ministry and, at other times, simply stand on the sidelines and watch, waiting for a time-out to offer suggestions.[2] Functioning in this capacity, the supervisors are tempted to engage in "disciple hunting," that is, to have the students model themselves in many aspects of pastoral care. Aware that this is one of the "special difficulties" involved in the supervisory process, they periodically examine their relationship to the students.[3] Aware that there is bound to be some modelling of supervisors, they periodically bring this to the students' attention. At the same time, they raise the issue of the modelling the students' parishioners do of them in their parish setting. Finally, they relate to the students as pastors conveying their concern for them as individuals and as students in process. Sometimes this is manifested by supporting them to give them the strength they need to continue their ministry. Other times it takes the form of confrontation, challenging them to use their full potential.

Because of the kinds of relationships between supervisees and supervisors, supervision differs from the classroom setting where teachers are usually viewed as persons who have all the answers, or where teachers pour all the right techniques into the students. It's also different from the classroom because the supervisees are pastors in the fullest sense of the word; they are fully responsible for those persons to whom they minister in the Clinical Pastoral Education Center.[4]

In addition to the relationship between students and supervisors, there are many other relationships in this educational context. Ekstein and Wallerstein use the clinical rhombus to illustrate some of these relationships. To convey their idea it is sufficient to modify their clinical rhombus as follows:

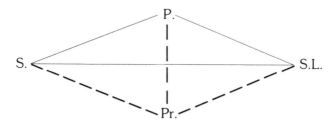

The "S" represents the student, the "S.L." the supervisor or leader, the "Pr." the president or administrator, and the "P" the patient or parishioner. Thus, there are several lines of communication, not just one. This rhombus could be expanded to include the staff, the patients' families, and the student's peers, because all of them are interacting with the student as she/he engages in a pastoral care education program. Such an enlarged rhombus would point out the complexities of interaction and communication and, consequently, the potentials of parallel process and problems in learning.[5] They also suggest potentials for transference and counter-transference. The full value of the rhombus is grasped when it is contrasted with the vertical line method of interacting as follows:

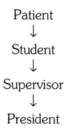

Patient
↓
Student
↓
Supervisor
↓
President

Two C.P.E. supervisors monitored an actual unit of Clinical Pastoral Education from the perspective of the rhombus. This demonstrated the complex psychological and social nature of the learning environment. They discovered from this unit that when they changed one part of the rhombus, it produced corresponding changes in the other parts. For example, they altered the patient (P) from the individual patient to each student's whole clinical assignment in ministry. This change provided an opportunity for evaluating the medical center's resources for pastoral education which made it possible for them to ask who they are in ministry. As a result, their paradigm shifted which created a change in the other parts of the rhombus. Once again this proved that a change in any part of an organization may impact on other parts or on the organization itself.[6]

Experiences

From interacting with all these various people, students gain many experiences. In a hospital setting, as they relate to nurses and other people who are caring for the sick in different capacities, they perceive people who are functioning in a very professional manner and who are confident and competent in their work. Some students are so overawed by this professionalism that their anxiety increases. Another result of interacting with these other professionals is that often it causes the students to reflect on their unique contribution to the patient's welfare as clergy persons. In addition, as the weeks go on, the supervisees see the human side of their professional peers and perceive them as imperfect, as not always giving the best care. This, in a sense, gives them permission to be less than perfect in their own ministry.

In ministering in this kind of setting, students experience some patients and their families who are joyous because the patients are preparing to be dismissed after successful surgery, and experience others who are very upset because the doctor has just informed them of a terminal illness. As a result, the students have the opportunity of rejoicing with one family and comforting the other in their sorrow. They encounter the "good patient" who never reveals any of his feelings and is eager to meet the expectations of the staff, as well as the "difficult patient" who is never pleased by anything the staff does. They minister to patients who have little or no knowledge of God, those who claim not to believe in God, and others who have an intense relationship with their Creator. They experience people who have the same value system as they do, and others who have a radically different one.

Reflection and Evaluation

In order for these experiences to be profitable, the students need to reflect and evaluate them. Writing verbatims is an excellent means to assist this process, because in so doing the students analyze their own response to determine their degree of effectiveness. The students check themselves to see where they switched the subject on the patient and reflect on their reason for doing so; they reflect on the appropriateness of gathering as many medical facts as possible from the patient; they evaluate "why questions" to see if they put people on the defensive; they determine the effectiveness of "closed questions" as opposed to "open-ended questions." Further, they evaluate their introduction to the patients when they enter their room to determine if it is conducive to effective ministry, and do the same with their manner of leaving the room at the conclusion of a visit. One student, for example, introduced himself in such a manner that it seemed as if he were apologizing for visiting patients. So he was asked to reflect on the value of his visit to the patient's welfare and challenged to reflect on his pastoral identity.

Students are assisted in the process of reflection and evaluation by their supervisor and peers. With this assistance the students are not only challenged to determine the reason some responses are ineffective, but also to reflect why others are effective. In addition, alternate methods of responding to patients and their families are indicated so that it becomes clear that there are a number of effective ways of ministering. Sometimes the patients, their families, and the staff enter into this process by giving the students feedback on their ministry.[7]

Emotionality

As students reflect and evaluate their ministry, they are given the opportunity to consider how their feelings or emotionality assist or block their ministry. Initially many students are unaware of the influence feelings have on ministry, and presume that ministry to the sick occurs simply through a head-to-head exchange with a patient or through prayer and Bible-reading. They miss the opportunity to interact on a person-to-person level. One student who was struggling with her own fear of cancer attempted to minister to a person who had the disease and who openly expressed his feelings of depression over his illness. The student became uncomfortable and tried to minimize her discomfort by switching the subject to some more positive aspects of his life, and urged the patient to be thankful "because you have such a wonderful wife to help you with your sickness." It is important to challenge the students to get in touch with their feelings about various kinds of illnesses so that they can be more effective in their ministry to the sick. It's especially helpful to them to acknowledge their true feelings about pain, bodily deformity, becoming dependent on others for the performance of the daily chores of routine living, of growing old, being forced into retirement, and dying.

In addition, students are urged to come to grips with their feelings in general in their interpersonal relations with their group, in their supervisory sessions, and in their many other interactions with people in the educational process. For most students this is difficult because of the low value our culture places on feelings. This difficulty is enhanced by many religious cultures which emphasize the tremendous value of the intellect over the emotions, and by the frequent restrictions religions have placed on the expression of "negative" feelings, e.g., anger or hatred.

When students realize how their feelings influence their ministry, they arrive at the "teachable moment." Jerome Brunner, in writing about the process of education, says that the task of teaching a subject to a person at any particular age is one of representing the structure of that subject in terms familiar to the person's own way of viewing things. Transferring this to supervision, it means that when the "teachable moment" comes, the student learns because supervisors or peers present the material in a manner congruent with the student's way of experiencing life.

Integration

In the educational process, students learn many techniques and theories about pastoral ministry in their classes and in the books recommended for their reading, but they are only beneficial if students integrate them into their personal and professional identities. Unless this occurs, these techniques and theories are merely extensions of the students who appear cold and wooden, using them in their ministry. Another effect of a lack of integration is that the convictions the students express have no depth. Patients quickly sense that the supervisees are simply speaking to them from the "head," rather than sharing "gut feelings." One student who had great difficulty in expressing anger, urged a patient to ventilate her anger because it would be helpful to her total well-being. Because of the student's own difficulties in sharing her anger, the patient did not perceive the expression as having any sincere conviction behind it. Generally, it takes months and years before some of these principles truly become part of persons and integrated into the totality of their being.

Further, students are challenged to integrate their entire educational experience with their theological principles so that the program is truly Clinical Pastoral Education. If this theological integration fails to occur, then there is little or no difference between a counseling program and a clinical pastoral program. As a result the students' theology and clinical work are compartmentalized rather than blended together, and often the students struggle with their identities as pastors. Students are enabled to integrate their theology with clinical experience by participating in morning devotions, by having a section of theologizing in each verbatim, and by having classes in theological reflection in which they analyze case studies in bioethics, e.g., determining to allow this baby to die or to perform any costly operations to enable him/her to live, examining the principles behind a student's decision to baptize this baby and not to baptize another, and reconciling a loving merciful God with tragedy.

Decision-Making

Finally, decision-making is an aspect of education, and the students' decision to embark on the educational pilgrimage is a significant one. Sometimes students seek acceptance in a program because some authority figure (e.g., the director of the lay pastoral ministry program) insists on it, and so reluctantly they commit themselves to it. If students maintain this attitude during the program, their lack of total commitment naturally affects their participation. They begrudgingly do their assignments, and display their hostility by turning in their assignments late and not presenting any material for the supervisory conferences. Before students begin, it's beneficial to urge them to reexamine the motives behind their decision "to sign up" for the program and to offer them a second chance to make the decision their own instead of someone else's.

Another significant decision for the students is to determine how much authority to claim for themselves and how much to give to their supervisor. Some students are so deferential, they claim no authority whatsoever and constantly seek advice from the supervisor regarding how to do this and that. Others adopt the attitude "nobody is going to tell me what to do" and so they are constantly rebelling. It is beneficial for students to examine their normal pattern of responding to authority to determine if they would like to change it. The students form a contract as the program begins in which they commit themselves to the general expectations of the program, and to discuss with the supervisor any particular aspect they find objectionable to see if some agreeable adjustment can be made.

The students continue to make judgments as the program proceeds. They need to decide whether they are going to take risks to grow or not. One student was fearful of the unknown, and so remained closed in spite of attempts to draw him out. Another student came with a burning zeal to develop her potential to the fullest and so tried new ways of relating to the patients, her peers, new methods of responding to feedback, and a new manner of interacting with authority. Students choose to relate deeply with people or only superficially, to have as many experiences as possible or just a few, etc. As the program comes to a close, they have to decide how they plan to use the knowledge and skills they have acquired. Some students, thrilled with their growth, plan to utilize their new skills in their ministry and intend to continue some kind of pastoral education in their own communities. Others decide one quarter of pastoral education is sufficient for their ministerial growth and aren't interested in any other programs.

It is essential that the students realize they have the power to make decisions in all aspects of their lives. No one forces them to become angry and throw things; no one forces them to marry or to choose celibacy; no one forces them to enter the field of pastoral care. These are options in life which they choose and they are responsible for their choices. Sometimes they are tempted to excuse themselves, blaming their parents or the spirit of our day for their actions. However, this is not valid. God gave all of us intellects and wills, and so we freely choose to do this and not that; we make decisions every day of our lives and have to take responsibility for them.

Finally, it is important for the students to realize they are responsible only for their own decisions and can't take responsibility for what others may decide to do or not to do. They aren't responsible because one of their patients chooses to remain depressed and makes no effort to adjust to the partial paralysis of his right side as a result of a stroke. Nor can students take full responsibility for the effect their decisions have on others. One student might choose to eat lunch with the nurses from his unit, while his peers resent this because they want all the students to share lunch together. This student is not responsible for the resentment his peers feel toward him, although he might have some responsibility to share the reason for his decision with them. Thus, students benefit from realizing they have only partial control over life and not complete control. A flyer advertising a set of cassette tapes (*Fully Alive*) illustrates these ideas very effectively. It follows on the next page.[8]

Conclusion

This educational theory presumes the existence of relationships, experiences, reflection and evaluation, emotionality, integration and decision-making. It presumes that because all these elements are present, the objectives of pastoral education can be attained:

1. Become aware of oneself as a minister and of the ways one's ministry affects other persons.
2. Understand and utilize the clinical method of learning.
3. Learn to make use of the peer group.
4. Utilize individual and group supervision for personal and professional growth and for developing the capacity to evaluate one's ministry.
5. Understand the theological issues arising from experience and enhance the interface between theology and the behavioral sciences.
6. Become aware of how one's attitudes, values, and assumptions affect one's ministry.

7. Become aware of the pastoral role in interdisciplinary relationships.
8. Become aware of how social conditions and structures affect the lives of others and of oneself.[9]

EXPERIENCE
YOURSELF

by getting
in touch with
and celebrating
your true self.

EXPERIENCE THE WORLD	EXPERIENCE GOD	EXPERIENCE THE MEANING OF LIFE
by deepening your awareness of the persons and things that daily touch the pulse of your life.	by exploring new pathways to a closer relationship.	by evaluating and clarifying your life values and goals.

EXPERIENCE
OTHERS

by discovering
the secrets
of communication
and loving listening.

Footnotes

[1] David A. Steere, *The Supervision of Pastoral Care*, Westminster/John Knox Press, Louisville, KY, 1989, pp. 30-31.

[2] Wayne E. Oates, *Pastoral Psychology*, "Pastoral Supervision Today," Fall, 1975, p. 24.

[3] Schuster, Sandt & Thaler, *Clinical Supervision of the Psychiatric Resident*, Brunner/Mazel, Inc., New York, NY, 1972.

[4] Wayne E. Oates, *op. cit.*, p. 28.

[5] Ekstein and Wallerstein, *The Teaching and Learning of Psychotherapy*, Basic Books, 1958, p. 138.

[6] Carole Somers-Clark and Logan Jones, "The Clinical Rhombus Revisited: Learning Through Resistance and Change," *The Journal of Pastoral Care*, Fall, 1993, pp. 207-215.

[7] David A. Steere, *op. cit.*, pp. 25-30.

[8] John J. Powell, S.J. and Loretta Brady, *Fully Alive* (Set of Tapes), Argus Communications, Niles, IL, 1980.

[9] Association of Clinical Pastoral Education, *Objectives of Basic C.P.E.*, 1993, p. 89, #123.2.

CHAPTER TWO

TOOLS USED IN SUPERVISION
OF PASTORAL EDUCATION

T HE GOAL OF PASTORAL CARE education is to enhance the pastoral care skills of the students so that they can be a companion to other people on their journey. This does not take place overnight, but rather occurs over a period of time with the assistance of a supervisor and some structure. The students need supervision, a process which enables them to evaluate their ministerial functions and their personal and pastoral identities. This is done with the supervisor, using his/her educational theory (the material presented in the previous chapter) as a guideline for the supervision. In Clinical Pastoral Education, the structure includes verbatim sessions, interpersonal groups, supervisory conferences, didactic sessions, a daily journal, midterm and final evaluations, and experiences of the students pastoraling patients and staff. They are assisted in this process not only by their supervisor, but also by their peers, the other professional staff, the patients, and their families.[1]

Initial Interview

Supervision begins with the initial interview which offers an opportunity to determine if the prospective candidate meets the criteria for admission, namely, sufficient educational background, emotional stability, pastoral identity, adequate motivation, and a willingness to be supervised. It is not necessary that the candidate be enrolled in the seminary, but that the person have some religious formation in a formal setting like that given to a deaconess, a woman religious in religious life, or a participant in a lay pastoral ministry program.

For the sake of the patients and the other participants in the program, it is important that the applicant be emotionally stable. Sometimes religious superiors who lack an understanding of the purpose of Clinical Pastoral Education (C.P.E.) refer their disturbed personnel, thinking it will be a substitute for therapy. Although there are some similarities between therapy and supervision, they are very different. If the major portion of time is spent with the student's inner problems, that is therapy. If the major portion of the time is spent discussing the patient's problems (even though some time is spent with the student's problems that are interfering with pastoral care), then it is supervision. If a student has some personal problems, possibly she/he could engage in therapy and at the same time be supervised in pastoral care in C.P.E.

A pastoral identity which separates the pastoral person from a social worker and a secular counselor is also important. One applicant, for example, said she did not believe in God and as a consequence never prayed. Such a well-intentioned person is not suited to function as a chaplain. During the interview the applicant is informed of the goals of the programs and the necessity of participating in the classes, verbatims, etc., and the supervisor attempts to determine if the prospective candidate has sufficient motivation to meet these and other demands of the program. Sometimes students apply for a program simply because they are told to do so, rather than because of personal motivation. Finally, the applicant needs to give evidence she/he is "supervisable," that is, open to change and growth, and is not intending to use the program only as a means to gain conversions to a particular denomination.

To assess whether the prospective candidates meet the admission criteria, they may be asked to describe their strengths and weaknesses or to give five adjectives that describe them and five others that do not. The candidates sometimes are asked to describe their mother or father to determine whom they model and to describe their present significant relationships and their support system. It is important too for them to relate some major event in their life and the meaning they attach to that. Finally, some are invited to describe how they handled conflict and anger recently in their lives. From the responses to questions like these, the supervisor knows if the persons can benefit from a C.P.E. program, something about their emotionality, and some of the supervisory issues that will occur. This initial interview also gives the individual prospective candidates an opportunity to evaluate the supervisor and C.P.E. program to determine if it is the best setting to promote their pastoral growth.

Supervision

Effective supervision requires a series of contracts. First there is the contract that arises between the supervisor and all the students. At this time there is a sharing of the expectations that the supervisor has of the students during the program. At the same time there are the legitimate expectations that the students have of the supervisor and the C.P.E. program. It is important that these expectations of one another be clarified so that everyone has the same understanding of them.[2] Another aspect of expectations is the learning contract that is established between the supervisor and the student. This will be discussed in the next section.

A vital part of supervision is the regular supervisory conference. It is important that this conference be structured so that it occurs on a regular basis rather than just occasionally. In this conference the students have the opportunity of asking questions about how to minister to certain patients, clarifying an aspect of some instruction that was given, reflecting together about some interaction in the interpersonal group, discussing some aspect of the daily journal of the students, and sharing ideas and feelings flowing from any aspect of the C.P.E. program or the student's personal life. This is the students' hour, and it is their opportunity to use this time for their personal and professional growth.

The supervisory conference provides the opportunity for the supervisor to check his/her emotional responses with the supervisee who does the same with the supervisor. In the academic sessions, it's a head-to-head interchange for the most part, while in the supervisory conference the emotions come into play. Both share their feelings and monitor them, trying to determine their cause. If a supervisor becomes sleepy during a supervisory session, she/he tries to determine the reason, e.g., because the supervisee is resisting, taking a "head trip," or because she/he never got enough sleep. In doing this, the supervisor makes a distinction between "old feelings" that she/he brings into the conference and "new feelings" sparked by the interaction with the supervisee. In one supervisory session, Joe began offering excuses for not having his verbatims in on time. He has done this before, blaming it on a broken typewriter, stalled car, etc. I was tired of this and shared my irritation with him. As a result, Joe stopped his excuses and simply said he was sorry he didn't have it. The next time when he began making excuses, I simply interrupted him and asked him to monitor what he was doing.

It is important for the supervisor and the supervisee to distinguish between supervision and consultation. In supervision the focus of attention is on the supervisee, while in consultation the focus is directed to the client of the consultee. William Barry illustrates this beautifully in an article in *Human Development* where he gives the following example. The consultee says, "I'm not sure what caused her state of depression." The response of the consultant, "Have you looked for a loss of some sort? Or perhaps a physical illness brought it on." In supervision, the supervisor says, "What were your thoughts and feelings?" Response of supervisee, "I couldn't understand his motives and I became increasingly afraid."[3]

During the supervisory process, the supervisor gains many insights into the students and is tempted to share them. However, this is only done if the supervisor intends to deal with these issues in detail. One student, Elizabeth, repressed her sexual feelings but I chose not to deal with them immediately and instead dealt with the goals she wrote for herself. Later when more trust was established and the timing seemed right, I challenged her in that regard.

An issue that often surfaces in supervision and generally in all aspects of the program is that of authority. The supervisees struggle to assume their own authority and to decide how much authority they will give to the supervisor. Another aspect of the authority issue is for the supervisor to determine how much authority the supervisor demands, and how much she/he encourages the students to own for themselves. The supervisor is aware of these authority issues, and lifts them up for the students in a manner and at a time that will facilitate their growth.

Learning Contract

Another tool of supervision is the learning contract which the students form in the first days of the program. An important part of the contract are the goals the students set for themselves. In a supervisory session these goals are discussed to determine if they are realistic, specific, and related to the goals of C.P.E. Sometimes students want to change them as a result of this discussion and other times the supervisor asks for a change. However, it's best to allow the students to keep their goals if possible, because they are more motivated to attain them if they are their own. Periodically the supervisor and the students examine the goals together to see if any changes are appropriate, and to reflect on the progress that has been made to attain these goals.[4]

Parallel Process

The students are assisted to achieve their goals when they allow the patients to become their teachers. This takes place when there is awareness of the parallel in the dynamics existing in the relationship between the supervisor and the supervisee, and in that existing between the supervisee and the patient. This is called the parallel process and it has two uses. First, as the supervisees relate to their supervisor, they relate to the patients. Joe usually avoided every question the supervisor asked him about his "negative feelings" as his verbatims were being examined, just as Joe constantly avoided feelings in his relationships with patients. Whenever the patients were on the verge of sharing their "negative feelings" about illness, he urged them to think positive. So as Joe related to his supervisor about feelings, he also related to patients to avoid them.

A second use of parallel process indicates that as the supervisor relates to the students, they in turn relate to their patients. Since students are relating to an authority figure, they might be more active or passive than usual. However, the parallel still exists and is a good teaching tool. I frequently confronted Mike about his avoidance of anger in ministering to patients, his tardiness in coming to class and in handing in verbatims. In relating to a 27-year-old female patient who had been very angry with her mother for 13 years, Mike confronted her concerning her continued anger, and asked her why she was unwilling to give it up. As I used confrontation in dealing with Mike, so he utilized it in ministering to patients.[5]

Affirmation and Confrontation — Means to Growth

To facilitate growth in the students, the supervisor uses a mixture of affirmation and confrontation. In my own growth as a person, I profited from both and think that other students do too. The supervisor affirms the students' unique strengths and reinforces what the students do that is effective in ministry. Having received this support, the supervisees are given the strength to lower their defenses and try new methods and new styles of behavior.[6]

From the New Testament we know that Christ is the perfect representative of the affirming person because he loved each person precisely as she/he was, yet at times he confronted people with their shortcomings. Christ affirmed Simon Peter when he professed his faith in him as the Messiah, the Son of the Living God, but later confronted Peter because of his denial, asking three times, "Peter, do you love me?" Christ mixed affirmation and confrontation in his interaction with the Samaritan woman at the well. He affirmed her by his acceptance of her which was indicated by his countenance and by gently engaging her in conversation, "Give me a drink." After she said, "I have no husband," Jesus confronted her in his reply, "You are right in saying you have no husband. The fact is, you have had five, and the man you are living with now is not your husband" (Jn 4:18). Thus Jesus accepted her as she was, and at the same time invited her to become a better person.

Resistance

Sometime during the program the supervisor usually meets resistance to personal and professional growth from the supervisees. This resistance which is conscious and unconscious is manifested when the students change the topic, relate a lengthy story, or fail to hand in their assignments. By these tactics they express a desire more to maintain the status quo than to risk the insecurity of change. On the one hand, the students want to learn, but at the same time are afraid to risk themselves. Even though trust has been established between the supervisor and the supervisees, this is not enough to overcome their resistance. Some information or suggested change is too threatening for the students to accept because it attacks their self-image, and so it is blocked out or interpreted in such a way as to pose less of a threat. All of us have perceptual screens which filter out or distort communication that makes us feel uncomfortable. Adults especially, have self-images that are more resistant to accept knowledge from others which demands a change.

To reduce the resistance the supervisor not only affirms the students' current strengths, but also identifies with them to bridge the gap between him/herself and the students. To do this, the supervisor and students seek out together where agreement exists among them, and then the supervisor helps them become aware of the feelings that appear to be behind the resistance. Often, it is fear directly or indirectly. The supervisor assists the students further by focusing on the work context, instead of on their differences. For example, Frank announced to the group he wasn't going to present any more verbatims because the group criticized him too much. To reduce his resistance I invited him to share his perception of the feedback on his verbatim. As he addressed that invitation, it was evident that he feared being criticized. After his peers interacted with him on that issue, I mentioned how awkward it would be for him to comment on his peers' verbatims and not to present any for them to comment on.

Students are assisted immensely in overcoming resistance if they become aware of resistance in one of their patients. Frank was helped when he encountered a patient who resisted his efforts to discuss cancer and his feelings about it. The harder he pushed her to talk about the life-threatening disease, the more she resisted. I pointed out the parallel to him between his patient's resistance and his own when Jean kept urging him to stop withdrawing from the group. The more she demanded he return, the more he avoided her.[7]

Searching for Options

Supervision enables the supervisee to seek and evaluate other options. When the supervisor functions in this way, there is no need to proselytize, nor to seek an extension of him/herself in the students. Rather, this approach enables the pastoral person to become a professional, to achieve self-realization. Such a supervisor is not tempted to over identify with the students because this kind of leader identifies with the process of supervision itself.[8]

An effective use of searching for options occurred with Jean. She came one week late for the program and during the first supervisory session asked how she could make up the time. Instead of giving her the answer, I asked her how *she* thought this could be done. She said she could stay a week after the program was over, but she didn't want to do this. Then she presented two other options, working after supper or on weekends. She chose some evenings and two Saturdays from the various options.

Pastoral Identity

The development of a pastoral identity is a crucial issue usually for pastoral persons because their pastoral effectiveness is severely hampered by a personal identity that is not integrated with their professional identity. If a supervisee's personal identity is arrested at a certain stage in his personality development, e.g., adolescence, then his incongruity expresses itself in anxiety. This anxiety is only a symptom of the real problem, the lack of an integrated pastoral identity.[9]

Role confusion also seems to stem from lack of a clear pastoral identity. A supervisee who has not struggled to attain his own pastoral identity easily adopts some of the roles of the other professionals with whom he works. In analyzing 150 verbatims over a two-year period, I discovered that a number of the students in C.P.E. programs in the hospital adopted the roles of (a) the medical person by asking and giving medical information, (b) the social worker by obtaining information about social security and nursing homes for the patients, (c) the "joyboy" by having a strong need to cheer up all the patients, (d) the problem-solver by listening to the patient's problem for a while and then offering a solution, and (e) the "super-professional" by hiding behind his/her profession with so much stiffness that the patient has no feel of the person as a human being.

Freud explains that the development of personal identity lies in the context of the family, basing it on the tender love of the parents for the child. Erikson develops his concept more fully and offers implications for the development of a professional identity.[10] Briefly, as the students grasp an understanding of their own emotional history, they comprehend their own continuity better which enables them to establish their personal identity. Their pastoral identity grows out of this personal identity, as well as out of an identification with some significant pastoral person, e.g., a supervisor or a pastor, and by engaging in pastoral responsibilities.

It is important to make a clear distinction between a program designed for psychiatric residents or students in social work and students in pastoral care. Sometimes students from all these programs are dealing with the same issues with a patient. Sometimes they are even using the same psychological tools, but the whole orientation is different with students in a C.P.E. program. Clergy persons have a pastoral identity while the others have medical or social identities. In order to communicate to the students the theological orientation of the program, morning devotions are helpful. More helpful are weekly theologizing sessions in which the participants are challenged to rethink their theological beliefs and to investigate whether they have a solid basis for a certain theological practice or opinion. So this process influences them to reread their theology so that they sharpen their thinking on various theological issues, and more importantly, it helps them to integrate their theology with their daily living. What value is theology if it is isolated from their day-to-day activities? Finally, this process challenges the participants to explain their theology to their supervisor and peers in clear terms.

The Supervisor as a Learner

The supervisor learns from using the parallel process. She/he learns by evaluating the effectiveness of her/his supervisory style with the supervisees during the program and as the program concludes. It is beneficial to offer the supervisees an opportunity to participate in such an evaluation. Finally, it is important for the supervisor to continue learning by pastoring patients in the setting where the supervision occurs. In doing this, the supervisor meets some of the personnel the students work with, continues to increase ministerial skills, and grows in understanding the students better, since she/he periodically will experience some of the same anxieties that the students do. So the supervisor is an educator, a pastor, and a learner. In order to facilitate this learning, the supervisor has available consultation because others (who are less close to the situation) often offer profitable insights.

In conclusion, an effective supervisor is an eternal learner, and as such helps the supervisees by identifying with their activity and process of constant growth, rather than with static opinions that have become frozen dogmas of limited usefulness. Supervising and learning are then mutually interdependent to maintain genuine professional identity.[11]

Footnotes

[1] Nash and Mittlefehdt, *American Journal of Ortho-Psychiatry*, "Supervision and the Emerging Professional," January 1975, p. 98.

[2] George F. Bennett, "Preparing Yourself for Supervision," *The Supervision of Pastoral Care* by David A. Steere, Westminster/John Knox Press, Louisville, KY, 1989, pp. 91-92.

[3] William A. Barry, S.J., "Supervision Improves Ministry," *Human Development*, Spring, 1988, pp. 27-30.

[4] John R. Compton, "The Supervisory Contract," *The Art of Clinical Supervision*, Paulist Press, Mahwah, NJ, 1987, pp. 41-52.

[5] David Steere, *op. cit.*, pp. 84-88.

[6] Conrad W. Baars, *Born Only Once*, Franciscan Herald Press, 1975.

[7] Melvin C. Blanchette, S.S., "Interpretation and Resistance," *The Art of Clinical Supervision*, Robert J. Wicks, Ed., Paulist Press, Mahwah, NJ, 1987, pp. 76-82.

[8] Ekstein and Wallerstein, *The Teaching and Learning of Psychotherapy*, Basic Books, 1958, p. 80.

[9] Max R. Maguire, Addresses and Workshop Papers, "Hang-Ups in Chaplain-Patient Relationship," "College of Chaplains," New Orleans, LA, January 13-14, 1969.

[10] Erik H. Erikson, *Childhood and Society*, W.W. Norton, New York, NY, 1950.

[11] Ekstein and Wallerstein, *op. cit.*, p. 80.

CHAPTER THREE

IDENTITY AND COMFORTABLENESS WITH FEELINGS

HERE IT IS ONLY THREE O'CLOCK and I'm finished! I visited the first half of the unit yesterday and saw the other 20 patients this afternoon." A statement like this is typical from a student beginning training in hospital visitation, because he is usually anxious about his visits and as a result generally makes very superficial, brief encounters. This same student told me six weeks later, "You shouldn't assign so many patients to the next group. I simply can't visit them adequately."

As his supervisor, I rejoiced in his growth because that comment and his verbatims (written records of his pastoral conversations with patients) indicated he was ministering on a deeper level with his patients. Consequently his visits took longer and were more beneficial. He had moved in his conversations from the "weather" and a superficial "how are you" to some real concerns because now he was relaxed, and as a result so were the patients. When he first began ministering at the hospital, the patients noticed his nervousness and so kept the visits short, for his sake as well as their own.

I have examined over 150 verbatims of some twenty students whom I supervised in Pastoral Care Education programs, and have noticed many common characteristics among them. I would like to share some of these with you and then draw a couple of conclusions.

Initial Anxiety Evident by Frequent Use of Questions

Since most of the students had little acquaintance with hospitals, it was normal for them to be anxious about their initial visits with sick persons. As the quotation at the beginning of the chapter indicates, some pastoral care students handled their anxiety by visiting many patients very briefly. Others coped with their anxiety by asking a number of factual questions so that there were no pauses in the conversation. One asked five factual questions as he began his conversation with the patient, and then relaxed enough to allow for a brief period of silence and for the patient to take the lead in the conversation. Another student who began the program with some skill in counseling, was able to relax more quickly and allowed the patient to take control of the conversation, indicating by his responses he was listening. He interacted with the 70-year-old patient who had been hospitalized more than a month for major surgery, in the following manner:

C-1: Hello, Mrs. X. Are you doing any better today?
P-1: Well, I'm all right... I guess. You know I've been out of bed and have been up and walking around.
C-2: Yes, I saw you in the hall yesterday and you seemed to be doing pretty well.
P-2: I guess I'll *have to be* discharged soon.
C-3: I'm sorry... I don't think I follow. You say you'll *have to be* discharged?
P-3: Well, if I'm discharged soon and I can't go back to my apartment... you know what that means?
C-4: No, not exactly, but go on, Mrs. X.

This interaction clearly keeps the focus on the concerns of the patient.

Forming a Pastoral Identity

Another problem that arises for many students deals with their pastoral identity. Seminarians are not alone in experiencing this difficulty; religious women and priests encounter similar problems, especially those entering the pastoral field from teaching or nursing. Some of us have never taken a good look at exactly who we are as persons. When people ask us who we are, the immediate response is "seminarian," "woman religious," "clergy person," or "a lay person." A minister never relates to a cancer patient, a lay chaplain never relates to a postman, and a housewife never relates to a teacher; but rather we relate to people who are religious women, clergy, housewives, and teachers. We don't relate to roles, rather to persons who have individual roles.[1]

Lay persons entering the field of pastoral care have to struggle with similar issues, but sometimes have a unique problem of viewing themselves as "chaplains" or "ministers." One student could not bring herself to introduce herself as chaplain to the patients because she was so steeped in the concept from her early training that only an ordained person is a chaplain. Unless our identity is clear as persons, we tend to be quickly aware of our insecurity when we encounter other people. In our uncertainty about our personal identity, we find it difficult to affirm other people in their personhood. So the real questions are: "Who are we personally? What are we feeling? What do we value highly? What do we disvalue? What relationships are important to us, if any? What are our natural strengths? What skills do we have? What are our weaknesses? What are our short-range and long-range goals?" It is important for all of us in pastoral care to know our emotions, relationships, strengths, weaknesses, values, and goals. Then we realize our personal identity; we know ourselves as persons.

Our personal identity is attained by receiving feedback from other people. If we are open to being affirmed by others, we understand our own goodness, we understand that we have certain gifts and can do certain things well. This means we are open to receiving compliments from other people. At the same time, our own identity is attained by rejecting the expectations other people place on us. This is especially necessary for clergy who are the object of great expectations from others because of their role. If we accede to the unrealistic expectations of others, then we adopt an "ideal self" and never discover the "real self." In addition to being open to having our goodness affirmed by other people, it's also necessary to accept the painful realization that we can't do everything. We have certain limitations, and that is acceptable. We are still good persons.

An authentic pastoral identity does not emerge from a fuzzy or fake personal identity. We must know who we are individually before we are ready to determine our pastoral identity, before we become aware of the role we want to exercise in the ministry, and before we discover how our functions differ from those of a nurse, doctor, social worker, or friendly visitor.

Another important factor in determining our pastoral identity is our model of Church. If our model is "institutional" with an emphasis on hierarchical authority, we will function differently than if our model is that of "servant" with an emphasis on love and service. Our pastoral identity will differ from both of these if our model of Church is that of "community." This model sees the Church not primarily as a visibly organized society nor as a group of persons seeking to be of loving service to others, but as a communion of persons united mainly by interior bonds of creed and ecclesiastical fellowship. Thus each model of the Church influences our pastoral identity and each has its strengths and weaknesses. It is profitable for us to be aware, as we form our pastoral identity, of which model or models of the Church upon which we rely most heavily.[2]

Confusion of Pastoral Identity

Because some students entered the program without having any insight into their pastoral identity, they immediately adopted the role of the medical person. They asked many medical questions of the nursing staff and attempted to acquire a quick course in medicine. In visiting patients, occasionally this role or confusion was so great that there was no difference between their visits and that of a medical resident. Unfortunately, it even happened that pastoral students delighted in their new knowledge and displayed it in the presence of the patient. One informed a patient why his surgery had to be postponed, instead of allowing a medical person to impart this information. The pastoral student said:

> When they ran the test, they found a slight fluctuation in your heart — something like an irregular rhythm in your heart beat. When your family doctor told them that you had this for a long time and that it would not affect the operation, they decided that it would be okay.

Other pastoral students perceived their pastoral identity as "problem solvers." They listened very carefully to discover the patient's problem and then offered a solution. Undoubtedly, many of them modeled themselves after their own pastors whom they saw function in this manner. Possibly, they were treated in this manner by their pastor when they were struggling with some difficulty, and so they adopted the same model of behavior. One patient who was hospitalized for rehabilitation therapy to gain the use of her legs was troubled when her 60-year-old husband suddenly began wearing very sporty clothes, bought a bicycle exerciser, and did not seem to want her to come home unless she could walk by herself. The student not only gave advice, but possibly raised new anxieties for his patient in his fifth interaction with her:

> It seems to me that your husband might be afraid of getting old. Both of you getting ill at the same time after many years of health and doing things together has been interrupted. I think he is afraid of being disabled. He has recovered from his condition and is trying to keep it that way. But a wheelchair at home is a reminder of what might happen to him.

Some of the students saw themselves as "cheerleaders," visiting patients to cheer them up. Nursing personnel often regard the chaplain in this light, saying "Mr. X. seems lonely today. You might try to cheer him up." At other times, the nurses express this idea in giving pastoral persons information concerning patients on the unit with special needs. "No, everybody seems pretty good today. Nobody is down." So, this role is placed on the chaplains and it's easy for them to accept it wholeheartedly if they don't have a strong pastoral identity. A side benefit from accepting this role is that the pastoral person thereby gains the acceptance of the nursing staff. One student used this approach so much that initially he seemed like a salesman. On closer examination though, it seemed that this was his way of gaining acceptance from his patients and a method he employed to keep the patients from discussing feelings, especially those of fear and anger.

In struggling to establish an identity, other students saw themselves as "persons of prayer" to the extent that they felt compelled to pray with every patient, whether the patient wanted a prayer or not. It appeared that pastoral persons thought they had failed to fulfill their duty unless they prayed with each patient. Briefly, these students had a far greater need for prayer than did the patients. One student stated her goal in the first minute of the interview:

> I've come to see you and to promise you my prayers, both
> this evening and tomorrow morning. If you wish, I'll pray
> a little surgery prayer with you now.

For some students, this essential element of their identity was "professionalism." Some stressed this so much they were incapable of expressing any warmth and seemed as though they were hiding behind their profession. One student constantly used the phrases "we think" and "we believe" and so I kept wondering in reading his verbatims what he personally thought about any given topic. This same student spoke to patients as though he were quoting from some textbook. His whole bearing was so professional that he was artificial, and there was no opportunity for the patient to see the real human being who was a pastoral person.

What a contrast these styles were to that of another student who was sure of his pastoral identity and walked with the patient in his pain. This student interviewed a 20-year-old university student, hospitalized for minor surgery and this is how the conversation flowed:

C-1: How's it going, Joe?

P-1: Pretty good, I'm pretty sure I'll be leaving tomorrow.

C-2: I guess you're kind of happy about that.

P-2: Yes I am. I'm kind of anxious to get back to work.

C-3: So that you don't fall behind?

P-3: Right... (a pause for a few moments)... You know I'd still like to talk to you about why I'm not practicing my religion.

C-4: Go ahead, Joe.

P-4: Well, it is not that I think religion isn't important, but I see people at church who are nothing more than hypocrites.

C-5: Hypocrites?

P-5: Yeah... they act like they're really holy.

C-6: And this phoniness you see really bothers you.

This student's clear pastoral identity enabled him to listen to the patient's concern, to encourage the patient to share it completely and to give the patient the feeling of being understood and accepted.

Discomfort With Feelings

One of the most common problems that some students experience is discomfort with the world of feelings. Since many seem totally unacquainted with their own feelings, they frequently become very uncomfortable when patients try to talk about how they are really feeling. In addition to having a clear pastoral identity, being comfortable with feelings is one of the most important aspects of pastoral care.[3] Sometimes seminary faculties and religious superiors denigrate feelings as they emphasize the value of the intellect. Students who took this approach were of limited help to patients initially because they could not enter their world of fear, pain, depression, anger, etc. One of the easiest ways of avoiding the feelings of the patient was simply to act as if they were not there. A student, who was very adept at sidestepping feelings generally followed a patient's expression of feelings with a factual question or statement. A 50-year-old widow who had to retire early because of a heart condition verbalized her struggle to adjust to the retirement and the student immediately responded, "Do you have any hobbies to occupy your time?" Another response which would have conveyed to the widow she was understood might be: "It seems this early retirement is really difficult for you to adjust to."

Other students used a little different approach to achieve the same goal. One student asked 13 questions in 15 responses and another asked 8 in 10 to stay in control of the conversation in order to stay away from any discussion of feelings. Another student pressed his own agenda in speaking with patients and also used prayers to attain his goal — discussing facts only. These students reminded me of an old TV detective program "Dragnet" in which Jack Webb played the part of the chief detective. He always appeared on the screen soon after some woman discovered a dead body and naturally was very upset. Jack Webb's famous response to this woman in distress was, "Just the facts, ma'am, just the facts." These students had their own indirect way of expressing the same wish — "just the facts, please no feelings."

After being in the program a few weeks, some students quickly became comfortable with mild, positive feelings. They were relaxed in comforting patients and families who were crying, were comfortable with brief silences, and were able to rejoice with those patients who were recovering successfully from surgery. However, it took quite some time before the students learned to deal effectively with anger or depression and other feelings which are often viewed as "negative." This is not surprising since our culture and early training often gave us the impression that these feelings were bad or not fitting, especially for Christians who have the assurance that the Good Shepherd will never leave us wanting. It takes time for us to become "whole" to the extent that we respect our feelings and those of others, even when they are negative.[4]

One patient whose doctor deprived her of cigarettes expressed intense anger toward her doctor to the pastoral student who replied: "You know, I'm wondering if your condition is more serious than you want to admit to yourself. Those cigarettes must be very bad for you." Clearly this response did not give the patient the feeling of being understood and accepted, but instead was an attempt to move the patient to the factual aspect of her condition.

Other milder feelings of this kind like fear and worry were avoided too by the students who displayed their anxiety not only by controlling the topics of conversation but also by attempting to control people — manipulating them into feeling how the clergy wanted them to feel. This tendency was especially common among those student who were former teachers. This is not surprising because for years they had been in a classroom struggling to keep control over the children and trying to mold them into good Christians. No doubt, at times they used manipulation to achieve this goal. In ministering to patients, some of them easily fell back into their old habit.

Attempting to manipulate patients' feelings to keep everything "nice" seems to be another trait for some former teachers. To keep things "nice," one former teacher told a 46-year-old man on the eve of his surgery, "When the report turns out good tomorrow, you'll be sorry you worried about the surgery." Another former teacher who was experiencing difficulty adjusting to the fact that she was no longer teaching teenagers told a 69-year-old widow, suffering intense pain over the past four years, "It's just silly to worry about taking medication to reduce the pain." This admonition was given, even though the patient expressed fear about the adverse side-effects drugs have on people. In addition to manipulating the feelings of patients, some former teachers had a tendency to "talk down" to patients as these examples indicate.

Discomfort With Discussing Death

In spite of all the programs on death and grief, there were still many students who were uncomfortable with these topics. They reacted to them like some of the other topics of a feeling nature — just like nothing significant had been said. Other students imitated some of the nurses and doctors in reacting to dying patients — they simply avoided visiting them or spent a very brief time with them. One pastoral person showed his uneasiness with a dying patient by standing some distance from him and avoiding touching his hand when that would have been appropriate. Others concealed their uneasiness, as this student did who in his verbatim simply avoided the topic when a 70-year-old patient opened the door to discuss it:

> Patient: I don't watch my diet as I should. But at my age I think I should be able to be a little careless if I want to. I have had a good life and am ready to go whenever the time comes.
>
> (pause)
>
> Pastoral Person: Are you feeling better today?

Other students were not only afraid of discussing death, but also any disease that might lead to that topic. One student had the technique of changing the subject when a patient spoke of cancer. On one occasion a woman mentioned to him in the hallway that she had just been informed that her husband had cancer. He carefully avoided the issue saying, "You are Mrs. X, aren't you? I met you the other day when I was visiting your husband. I am sorry that I did not recognize you away from your husband." If patients are going to receive effective ministry, we in pastoral care need to invite them to discuss any topic.

Discomfort With Intimacy

Another characteristic I noted in many students was their discomfort with intimacy. Some have not revealed much of their personal lives to anyone, and so were anxious when patients begin pouring out their innermost secrets to them. They simply didn't know how to handle this kind of sharing. Some attempted to ease their nervousness by changing the subject, as one student did when his patient mentioned she was living in sin since she was married outside her church. Other times they simply expressed their shock to the patient, as happened when a woman confessed that her husband, a confirmed alcoholic, went to a bar sometimes and just stayed there until he was completely drunk. The student responded: "Is his problem that bad?" A more pastoral response might have been, "I wonder how you're dealing with this."

Conclusion

I have generally mentioned instances from verbatims of students where their lack of a clear pastoral identity, of an awareness of their own feelings, and of an ability to minister to the feelings of patients has hindered their pastoral effectiveness. However, there were many other occasions where they interacted effectively with the sick. For example, after a 53-year-old lady told a student she had suffered much in her life, he felt comfortable enough to walk with her in her pain by asking her a very open question, "How has your suffering affected you?" After some weeks in the program, another student felt comfortable with silence and viewed it as profitable time for the patient to think and come in touch with his feelings. Because of this, he simply remained silent as he nonverbally displayed his concern for a 66-year-old man who said, "I received some bad new today, but it's hard to put it into words."

Sometimes, too, students were appropriately assertive with patients by not allowing them to drift from one topic to another and by urging them to share their feelings. The evening before surgery, one patient mentioned he was upset about the operation, but failed to say more about it. The woman chaplain responded, "Would you like to talk more about what upsets you concerning tomorrow's surgery?" This invitation indicated she was comfortable to be emotionally available to the patient.

Fr. Henry Nouwen has urged pastoral care persons to be compassionate in our ministry to manifesting our human solidarity as we cry out with those who suffer, to console patients by feeling deeply the wounds of life, and to offer comfort by pointing beyond the human pains to glimpses of strength and hope. He went on to say that the greatest compliment we can receive from a patient is, "That person really understands me and, as a result, I feel comforted."[5]

Footnotes

[1] Bernard J. Busch, "Intimacy and the Celibate Life," (tape) Kansas City, MO, *National Catholic Reporter*, 1978.

[2] Avery Dulles, *Models of the Church*, Doubleday and Co., New York, 1978.

[3] Philomena Augudo, "Religious Women as Pastoral Ministers," *Emmanuel*, Dec. 1978, pp. 59-34.

[4] Molly Young Brown, *Growing Whole*, Harper Collins Co., New York, 1993, pp. 11 & 12.

[5] Henry Nouwen, "Compassion: Solidarity, Consolation and Comfort," *America*, America Press Inc., New York, NY, March 13, 1976, pp. 195-200.

CHAPTER FOUR

FEELINGS

I N MINISTERING TO ANOTHER, we relate to the whole person with our whole person. We don't relate simply as professionals. Rather in ministry, our whole being becomes involved, and this includes our feelings and the feelings of the people to whom we are ministering. We relate to the other members of the healing team too, and this means we relate with our feelings as well as theirs. (I wish to credit John L. Wallen, Ph.D. for the seminal thoughts present in this chapter.)

Dealing with these feelings of ours and those of other people is the greatest source of difficulty in our interpersonal relationships in ministry. This is a very broad statement, but it can be supported if we reflect on various incidents in our own lives. How often when we began describing how bad things were going for us, did we hear the phrase, "Cheer up, don't let it get you down," or "It's silly to feel that way." Three people told me after my 90-year-old father died, "He lived a long life. You shouldn't be sad about his passing." Pastoral persons who are having difficulty dealing with their feelings after ministering to a family after a tragic death might say, "I don't know why I feel this way but... ," or possibly in an argument it is said, "Let's keep emotions out of this and look at it more rationally, let's try to be more objective." It seems that we spend a lot of time and energy trying in one way or another to ignore or deny our own feelings, or the feelings of others. Actually, we are having feelings every day of our lives, but we tend to view them as upsetting. In effect, we are saying it's a problem being human because we are experiencing human feelings.

Another reflection supporting our difficulties with feelings is to examine how often we share feelings directly with the person about whom we are experiencing them. We mention to our friend that we are very angry because our boss reprimanded us, or that we feel loving and grateful toward our boss because he went out of his way to do us a favor. But notice that we are not telling that particular person our angry or loving feelings, but verbalizing them to someone else. Another aspect of this issue is the time perspective. When did those feelings occur? Often we find few discussions of feelings which a person is presently experiencing in comparison with the number of discussions about past feelings. A person might say, "One month ago when you told me you weren't going on vacation with me this year, that really hurt me." This person is relating a feeling, but it is a feeling that is four weeks old. If we look at the way we human beings interact with one another, we will discover that we ignore feelings by talking to someone else about the feelings we have toward a particular individual or by talking about past feelings. Dealing with feelings, mine and other people's, is the greatest source of difficulty in interpersonal relationships in ministry.

The first characteristic of feelings is that people tend to identify feelings with intentions. If some action of another person is an occasion of our anger, we attribute ill intentions toward him/her and on the contrary, if an action of another pleases us we attribute loving intentions to that person. When someone allows a door to slam in our face, we tend to attribute thoughtlessness to him/her or think he/she is angry at us for some reason. In reality though, the person might be totally unaware we are behind him/her, yet our tendency is to attribute ill-will toward that individual. On the other hand, there is the tendency to attribute good intentions when another person's action makes us feel good. Recently I went to buy a pair of shoes, and while I was trying on the shoes the salesman began telling me how shoes were made and the six possible measurements for a shoe, not just the measurements in the length and width. My initial feelings were very warm toward this salesman for taking the time to explain those interesting facts about shoes, because I judged he was being extra kind to give me that useful information. However, ten minutes later he told me quite frankly that he gave me all this information while the new shoes were on my feet so that he could convince me of the shoe's comfort and quality. Then I realized he was being kind to me simply to make a sale, and so I ceased attributing positive intentions to him.

A second characteristic of feelings is that they serve "a fuse function." Feelings tell us what an individual situation means to us. Feelings tell us whether we are comfortable or uncomfortable, loving or hateful, fearful or relaxed. If we look at an electrical switch box in our homes and find a fuse burned out, the fuse tells us there's something wrong in the circuit. We check it out to see where the overload is, correct that error, and then replace the fuse. The fuse tells us we have overloaded the circuit before the whole house burns down. Feelings serve a similar function in our interpersonal relations, in the sense that before the relationship is destroyed completely, we feel resentful; before a situation is at the breaking point, we feel angry. These feelings are signals indicating that in order to sustain a relationship, we have to check out and examine what is occurring presently between us and another person.

A third characteristic of feelings is that we can focus on them or focus elsewhere. Our power of attention enables us to some extent to select one feeling to concentrate on and to reject another one. If someone urges us to focus on the pressure our watch is exerting on our left wrist, we are aware of it; but before anything was said it was in the margin of our attention. The focus of our attention can change, if someone says, "Be aware of the fingers on your right hand." These fingers were here all the time, but we weren't thinking of them before. Our attention has shifted from the watch on our wrist to the fingers on our right hand. No doubt, one can refuse to be aware of the sensation on one's wrist or the fingers of one's right hand, but one can only refuse to focus on these parts of one's body if one intentionally focuses on someone or something else. This is what happens when we ignore our feelings, we repress them.[1] Over the years we formed the habit of diverting our attention from feelings to something else. If the cast on our broken leg is itching and we turn the TV on to watch the Super Bowl football game, we soon forget our uncomfortableness because during the game our attention is focused on our favorite team. As long as we are absorbed in the game, we are unaware of the itching, yet the cast is on the leg all the time.

We can do the same thing when we make judgments about other people, instead of being aware of our real feelings, focusing our attention on someone else instead of on ourselves. If our supervisor criticizes us, we may feel inadequate and resentful. But instead of focusing on ourselves and our unpleasantness, we focus on the supervisor, saying he/she is unfair and stupid. By judging the supervisor, we are trying to take away our uncomfortable feelings. We deny our feelings because they are expressed as his/her characteristics. By making judgments about another, we keep our feelings in the margin of our attention. Whether feelings are in the focus or in the margin of our attention, they still influence our behavior.

Finally, feelings cannot be controlled by leaving them outside of the focus of our attention. We can only control feelings by leaving them in the focus of our attention and using them to help us diagnose what's going on in the situation right now. For example, a friend called an hour before dinner and asked if he could come to eat with us at the hospital. I said that it was OK, even though I was irritated because I told him on a couple of occasions that the cook needs two hours notice to conveniently prepare for another person for supper. My friend came for supper, and after we finished eating, he commented, "This really upset you that I gave you such short notice, didn't it?" I was surprised by that question and asked him how he gained that insight. He replied that initially during the meal I talked constantly with the other hospital chaplain and did not draw him into the conversation at all. I displayed my irritated feelings nonverbally, and did not control them by putting them out of the focus of my attention.

Sometimes there is great emphasis on control and being in control of ourselves as an indication of our maturity. We tolerate a child having a temper tantrum because he's only five, but we look down upon an adult who has a temper tantrum. However, it's foolish to think that feelings can by controlled by ignoring or denying them. When we do this, we give up control and allow them to control us. If we feel angry and convince ourselves we don't feel angry, this simply means we've trained ourselves to ignore a set of feelings, to repress them. We can repress our feelings of anger or sexuality, but they still affect our behavior. The method to control our feelings is to be aware of them, to experience them consciously. Then we can control the behavior flowing from the feelings. Therefore, we need to value our feelings, to respect them as we strive to understand what they are telling us about a situation, other people or ourselves.[2]

Five Basic Emotions

This concept of awareness of feelings is understood more clearly by examining the physiological aspect of the five basic contact emotions. When we are angry, our body sends us a clear message communicating our anger. We want to fight physically or possibly verbally; our whole system tells us so because we breathe faster, our heart beats faster, our muscles begin to contract, and we actually have a sensation of heat. When we are fearful, almost the opposite bodily reaction to anger takes place. Our mouth becomes dry, we feel cold, our palms begin to sweat, and we have a desire to run away. If we shake hands with someone who is frightened, the cold sweat is quickly evident. When we feel hurt, we withdraw and regress as if we wanted to go back into our mother's womb. A common symptom of hurt which we all recognize is crying. However, many of us find it very difficult to display our hurt because in the minds of many people that means we are weak. Women often feel more freedom to express their pain through tears than men. Another fundamental feeling is trust. When we are open with someone, we are saying, "I am comfortable in your presence to the extent that I'm willing to be vulnerable." The opposite of course is mistrust, a feeling of not being free, not being able to be ourselves with one another. When we are not trusting, we hold back and our friends never know what we are feeling or thinking.

The final basic emotion is love, and again our bodies tell us physiologically whether we are feeling lovable. When we are loving, there is a warm glow about us which we can easily compare to anger which is a hot emotion. The two feelings are similar. In order to express love we have to take the risk of first expressing the other four feelings, and this means we can never have a true lasting relationship with another until we are able to fight with that person. When we are able to display our anger toward another, our fear, our hurt, and our trust — then we can love. When we can level with each other, telling each other how we feel and allowing our feelings to be shared openly, then we can experience closeness. Thus, love is a fulfillment of all of these other feelings.[3]

If we are struggling to get in touch with these basic emotions we can take comfort in the fact that the famous psychologist, Carl Rogers, once admitted that he has had difficulty with some of them. He said he was brought up in a situation where anger was simply not a feeling to be exhibited or expressed. As a consequence when it did come out, it was pretty violent. He acknowledges that over the years, he has become more and more aware of the times when he is angry but sometimes he is not aware of it at the moment it is occurring. Another emotion that Carl Rogers admitted he had difficulty talking about and struggled with for a long time was a feeling of warmth and love from others. He admitted that it was hard for him to feel good about himself and to understand how others could praise him so highly for something he did.[4]

Levels of Communication

It is valuable for us to be aware of the different levels of communication between people.[5] The first represents the lowest level of communication. At this stage there is no communication unless it happens by accident. People interact very superficially and exchange cliches with one another such as, "How are you? How is your family? How is your job?" Generally people are not really interested in the answers to these questions and are astounded if you ever take such a question seriously and begin answering in detail. Usually the person senses the superficiality and the conventionality of our concern, and obliges us by simply giving the standard answer, "O.K." This is the kind of conversation that takes place at cocktail parties, at reunions and meetings. There is no real sharing of persons, and everyone remains at a safe distance from one another.

On the second level there is reporting the facts about others. In this level there is no sharing of anything about ourselves but rather we talk about others, remaining content to tell others what we read in the newspaper. There is no personal commentary on these facts, but simply a reporting of them. On this level there is a seeking for shelter in news items about others. There is no giving of anything of ourselves and no invitation for others to give in return. Here we might share some facts about a proposed national health plan, but don't say what we think about it.

In the third level some communication of the person occurs. We are willing to risk telling something of our ideas and revealing some of our judgments and decisions. Here we can point out what aspects of a national health plan we like and what aspects we dislike. As we communicate our ideas though, we are watching carefully to test the trust level of the other person. We want to be sure the other person will accept our ideas, judgments, and decisions. If the other person raises their eyebrows or narrows their eyes, if the person looks at his/her watch, we usually retreat to safer grounds. We begin saying things we suspect the other person wants us to say, and try to be what the other wants us to be.

In the next level the participants have the courage to share their feelings, and some gut level sharing takes place. Here we go beyond revealing our ideas, decisions, and judgments; we differentiate ourselves from others by communicating our own feelings about these matters in our lives. In this level we really want others to know who we are, and so we share from our gut as well as our head. At this point we might share how fearful we are of the details of a health plan or how delighted we are with them. Many people share ideas and judgments, but the feelings that underlie them are uniquely ours. No one is committed to a political party or to a cause with our exact feelings of fervor or apathy. No one experiences our passions, senses our frustrations, or labors under our apprehensions. On this level we wish to share with others these feelings if we are to reveal who we really are.

When our own reactions are completely shared by a friend, when our happiness or grief is perfectly mirrored in him or her, we have attained the highest level of communication. We are like two musical instruments playing exactly the same piece of music in perfect harmony. In this peak communication which exists among close friends or between partners in marriage, there exists from time to time a complete emotional and personal union, in which one opens oneself in such a way that the other is called out of oneself and out of one's old and fixed positions into a new beautiful experience. In our human existence this can never be a permanent experience, but there are moments when an encounter attains perfect communication.[6]

Methods of Sharing Feelings

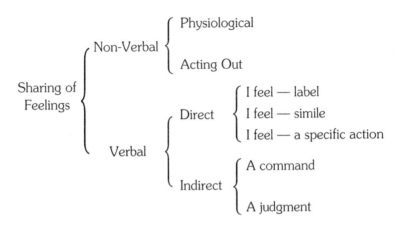

We often communicate our feelings nonverbally in a physiological manner when we realize we made a mistake. We feel embarrassed and our face becomes flushed. This is a physiological nonverbal communication of our feelings. Another manner of non-verbally communicating feelings is "acting out." Frequently nurses use this phrase on psychiatric wards, describing a patient as acting out her anger by throwing dishes on the floor in the cafeteria. In our lives we "act out" our love or forgiveness by hugging a person or our anger by clenching our fist at them. After an Interpersonal Group Session in which a woman became very hurt by what a man said, she forgave him after sharing her hurt by offering to hug him.

There are also many ways of verbally communicating feelings. The most effective method is a direct reporting of feelings which is done in three different ways. First, we use the word feel followed by a particular kind of feeling or a label. For example, I feel happy, hopeful, sad, mad, glad, angry, hurt, etc. Sometimes we vary this form by simply stating a feeling word and not using the word "feel" — I am happy, hopeful, sad, etc. Another method of reporting feelings is to use the phrase, "I feel like" with a simile. For example, I feel like a little boy who has been spanked, or I feel like a king, meaning that someone has treated me with special kindness. A final way is to follow the phrase, "I feel like" with some particular action. I feel like hugging you, indicating my affection; or I feel like running away, sharing my fear. All of these three methods of expressing feelings directly give people clear messages about us.[7]

When we report our feelings directly, it's helpful to do so in such a manner that our friend doesn't feel coerced to change. Our message is not "I'm scared; slow down," but rather it is "I'd simply like to inform you that I'm scared." A person who is sincerely interested in us will consider that.

There are indirect expressions of feelings, but these messages are not as clear. These occur when a person gives a command and hidden underneath that expression is a feeling. A teacher in a classroom shouts, "Shut up" and beneath that expression the students know there is anger. One may shout at a friend, "Go fly a kite."

Underlying that command, the friend feels the anger. Another method of indirectly expressing feelings is done through a judgment. Instead of being aware of our feelings, we focus our attention on our boss or a friend who has offended us. We say that Tim is stupid or insensitive, and beneath those expressions are feelings of hurt or possibly inadequacy. Perhaps the most frequent indirect expression is made by a frightened passenger in an automobile when the driver is speeding. Instead of saying, "I'm scared" which is a clear reporting of feelings, the passenger beats around the bush with his vague communication, "Do you think it's safe to drive this fast?"

Frequently we report feelings vaguely. (I am aware of the struggle that exists in my own life in being straightforward.) This happens because we are not only uncomfortable with feelings in general, but because we have feelings about our own feelings. If as a child we threw a book at our brother in an angry argument, our parents probably scolded us for doing this. Unfortunately the message we probably picked up is that throwing books and anger are both bad. So we develop feelings about anger and guilt. A young girl of seven who was very affectionate with relatives at a family gathering and criticized for it, learned not only that it is wrong to express feelings of affection, but also learned to be anxious about feeling affectionate. As an adult she struggled to allow feelings of affection to come into the focus of her attention, but preferred to keep them in the margin of her awareness. She has a feeling about her feelings of affection, anxiety.

Another factor concerning our difficulty in sharing feelings is that at times we have ambivalent feelings toward others. I remember feeling very grateful and loving toward my dad, but at the same time feeling irritated when at 82 years of age he tried to cut the front and back grass in one afternoon in 90 degree weather. Possessing loving and irritating feelings simultaneously tended to confuse me, until I realized it's possible to have conflicting feelings at the same time.

Andy Rooney on the *60 Minutes* TV program illustrated how to live comfortably with conflicting feelings. After his long time friend Harry Reasoner died of cancer of the lungs, he spoke about him on the regular Sunday night program. He mentioned what great work Harry Reasoner did, and how close they had become working together for a number of years. He clearly shared his conflicting feelings, "I miss him, I loved him, but I'm angry with him because he continued smoking even after his diagnosis of cancer and all the announcements about smoking being linked to cancer."

Value of Sharing Feelings

Even though it's valuable to report our feelings clearly, still we may have difficulty in doing this because of previous training. Generally Christianity has a reputation for urging caution in regard to feelings and emphasizing the value of the intellect as a faculty that would lead us more safely to God. This was particularly true in religious communities and seminaries where close friendships were forbidden or strongly discouraged. These were viewed as possibly leading to forbidden sexual activity, or at least as being disruptive of community life. Because of this kind of training, we sometimes relate to others only through our roles. Possibly because of our anxiety to protect ourselves and our failure to risk, we hide behind our Roman collar or our religious identity and don't relate as persons, abstracting from our own roles and functions. We relate to others only in a professional manner, and allow them to know nothing of what is behind that professionalism. Today, though, there is a more positive view toward intimate friendships where there is a deep level of sharing. Many spiritual writers view intimate friendships as a stepping stone leading to a deep union with Almighty God.[8] It is important for religious persons to be able to develop these kinds of relationships, and an essential element to that goal is an ability to share one's feelings. Intimacy demands communication on an intellectual as well as an emotional level, and the most difficult feelings to relate are those of hostility, anger, and love.[9]

To appreciate the value of sharing our feelings, we might reconsider the first sin of humankind. God gave Adam a command to share and reveal himself to Eve, and gave Eve a similar command to share and reveal herself to Adam. However, instead of revealing and sharing themselves, they decided to be mysterious, to hide from each other, to put on masks and to deceive one another concerning who they really were. Instead of openness and sharing entering into the world, deceit, mystery, and sin entered the human family. This resulted in isolation of one person from another, and ultimately isolation of the human family from God.

Obviously, one of the primary benefits resulting from sharing on a deep level is a close relationship with another person. There is a real meeting of the other person where he/she lives. Another benefit is that we have the warm feeling of being understood and of being supported. There is an equal opportunity for us to understand and support the other person, which produces an enjoyable feeling. A third benefit is that it helps us to discover some patterns of immaturity on our part, to gain insight concerning some aspect of our personalities that we might want to change. Because this is said openly, we not only know it, but have the courage to risk changing. If we consistently seek out friends for the sake of support, sooner or later the question arises why we need so much support. We may come to the realization that we don't accept the compliments people give us and value ourselves more highly. A fourth benefit of this type of communication is that it tends to create honesty and openness in others. Because we are open and honest, other people tend to follow our example. Because we are willing to risk sharing our feelings, another person feels free to trust us to share his.[10]

Deep communication makes our ministry effective because it enables us to deal with our feelings before we attempt to minister to others' feelings. When we enter into a patient's room, it is important that we leave our baggage outside. This means that we deal with our feelings of fear of cancer, of dying, and of tubes before we enter that room. If we are very fearful and try to repress our fears as we are interacting with the patient, our energy is being used in repressing our fears and not in being present to the patient. There are also occasions when it is important to deal with our feelings while we are interacting with the patient. Sometimes while we are visiting a patient, feelings suddenly rise within us. One method of dealing with those feelings is to share them with the patient. "Your cancer frightens me too, and just as you don't know how to respond to it, I don't know how to respond to you as you tell me that today the doctor gave you the bad news that you do have cancer." Molly Young Brown has some helpful hints on how to deal with fear in her book *Growing Whole*.[11]

Sharing Gut Level Communications

While the value of sharing gut level communications has been endorsed, there need to be certain guidelines concerning their use.[12] The first guideline is that gut level communication never implies a judgment of the other. It is simply unreal to expect we can judge the intention or motivation of another. We need to be realistic enough to admit the mysteriousness and the individuality of another human being, and thereby realize we cannot know that person's motivation. We don't have X-ray eyes, and the only way we can know another person's intention is to ask. When we are emotionally honest with another person, there is no judgment present. If we say, "I am irritated with you," we are being emotionally honest and are not implying in the least that it is another's fault that we are annoyed. We are not saying it is anyone's fault, but only reporting our feelings toward the person at this time. Perhaps it is our own "hang-up" on authority or our own irritation with our life that causes us to be annoyed. Let's take another example. "I feel hurt by what you said." Again we are not implying any judgment. Perhaps, we have difficulty dealing with differences and this makes us feel hurt. Or perhaps, we have feelings of inferiority and so need a great deal of support. When we don't receive that support, we feel rejected and hurt.

The second guideline is that emotions are good. All feelings are good. They are not indifferent and certainly not bad in themselves. God created our feelings to help us live a rich, full life. Moral values cannot be placed on sexual urgings, anger, trust, etc. However, they can be placed on the actions that flow from these particular feelings. We have been taught that certain feelings are good and others are bad; some are acceptable and others are unacceptable. The truth is that feelings are simply a part of being a human person, and sin only enters the picture depending on what we decide to do with the feelings we are experiencing.[13]

Today in some encounter groups there is a heavy emphasis on getting in touch with one's feelings and in sharing all feelings with everyone. While sharing is encouraged, total sharing with everyone is inappropriate because this is spiritual exhibitionism and can be harmful. When this philosophy of total sharing of all feelings is put into practice by two depressed people, the result can be disastrous. One person says, "Everything is going wrong and I'm depressed" and the other person responds, "I'm depressed too. Let's commit suicide together." One person adds to the other person's depression by his inappropriate sharing. There is equal emphasis in some groups on "acting out" one's feelings, but no emphasis is placed on responsibility for those actions. The message here is "if it feels good, do it." Certainly this kind of behavior is discouraged just as strongly as repressing feelings. However, in the third guideline, integrating our feelings with our intellect and will is endorsed. Such an integration indicates our maturity, while our immaturity is manifested by allowing our feelings to control our life. It's one thing to admit we feel sexually aroused by a particular person, and an entirely different matter to attempt sexual activity with that individual.[14]

In the interplay between feelings, intellect, and will it is important to realize that our intellect helps us to be aware of the feelings we are experiencing and that this is an asset to us. The intellect, in turn, presents these feelings to the will so that appropriate decisions are made. There is a beautiful interaction between feelings, intellect and will and we do not place more value on the intellect than on feelings, nor do we place more value on feelings than on the intellect or the will. All three are very important for functioning effectively as a human being.

The fourth guideline is that gut feelings are usually reported. If we wish to share ourselves with another, then we reveal our feelings whether we intend to act upon them or not. We share our anger with our friend without implying in any way that she is the cause or that we intend to hit her. We share our feelings of love without implying that we intend to engage in sexual activity with that person. If we are to open ourselves to another, we allow that person to experience us as we are; we share with her our hurts, our fears, and our love. Recently a doctor friend of mine who was a hospital patient beautifully illustrated this before his operation for removal of a cancerous tumor. On the eve of his surgery he broke down and cried in my presence saying simply, "I'm scared." Thereby, he shared himself with me.

Psychosomatic medicine indicates that many illnesses are caused by repressed emotions that find an outlet through headaches, skin rashes, allergies, asthma, common colds, aching backs or limbs, high blood pressure, etc. This means we are unable to bury emotions. They remain in our subconscious minds and intestines to harm us. It is not only conducive to deep friendship to share our true feelings, but it is equally beneficial to good health.

The most common reason offered for not wishing to share our feelings with our friends is that we don't wish to hurt them. However, we hurt our friends by not sharing ourselves with them openly. Another fear we have in sharing our feelings with others is that we suppose people will reject us because some emotions might be viewed as unacceptable. As was mentioned earlier, we have feelings about some of our feelings. We are ashamed of some of them, and rationalize that we cannot share them because they would be misunderstood or disturb a peaceful relationship. These reasons are not valid, because any relationship that is built on anything less than openness and honesty is built on sand.

The fifth guideline is that with rare exceptions emotions are reported at the time they are being experienced. It is much easier to report a feeling we had two weeks ago or two years ago, rather than to admit right now we are very angry with a friend. When we have the courage and honesty to share our feelings at the time they are occurring, then our relationship can achieve a high degree of intimacy, and indicates there is a high level of trust between us.

Emotions are like a good glass of wine which we savor and drink very slowly. We become deeply aware of the feelings that we are experiencing and know them in the depths of our being. Then we decide how we are going to share them and when we are going to share them. Occasionally, it is inappropriate to share the feelings here and now because a person cannot accept them. If a friend is preparing to go into the sanctuary to lead a service, it might be inappropriate to share our anger at that time because of something our friend did a few moments ago. Our intellect and will come into play in deciding how to share our emotions. If we become extremely angry with a friend, our emotional urge might be to hit him, but our will guides us to express our anger in a manner to facilitate our relationship rather than destroy it.

Not only between friends are there rare occasions when we would defer sharing of our feelings, but there are exceptions to this rule to defer or eliminate the reporting of our feelings in the case of a passing incident with a person we hardly know. The irritation we feel when a driver on the highway cuts us off might be better kept to ourselves. In the case of two persons who work or live together, or want to relate deeply with one another, this emotional reporting at the time that the feelings are experienced is essential.

Conclusion

Many of us are quick to respond to situations intellectually and never look inward to see what our real reactions and feelings are. A husband and wife in a married couples' group had a disagreement. In their interaction the moment the husband finished talking, the wife was right there with her statement which did not allude to his at all. She was constantly waiting for a pause in order to give him her response. A group member stopped her short and said, "Did you hear what he said?" She responded, "Of course I did." However, when she was asked to recall what he said, she thought and thought but embarrassingly could not give any hint of his statement. Then she turned to her husband and finally said, "What did you say?" In other words, she not only did not listen to his ideas, but she never listened to the feelings behind those ideas because her own attitude at those times was, "I'll win the argument over you, I'll get in my two cents worth that will be much better than what you have just said." She was totally unaware of this. In order to minister effectively to other pastoral care persons and people in our various settings, we have to listen, not only to their ideas but to their feelings.

Many people are unaware of their feelings at the time they are occurring, but they may become aware of them much later. It takes practice and self-training to ask: "What is my feeling at this moment? Am I frightened? Am I anxious? Am I angry? Am I feeling affectionate? Am I sad? Am I pleased?" Sometimes we know we are feeling something, but don't know exactly what it is. We have to give ourselves a moment or two to find out. Initially, getting in touch with our feelings is done quite consciously and then gradually it becomes automatic. It becomes automatic to look inward to recognize what we are feeling, and then to be willing to express it in almost all interpersonal relationships. Aware of our feelings, we can use them very constructively in our interpersonal relationships with our fellow ministers and with the people to whom we are attempting to minister.

By being in touch with our feelings, we can also be in touch with certain beliefs that underlie these feelings. As a clergy person, for example, we may believe we should be respected. When courtesy is not shown us, we feel angry and hurt. Being aware of these feelings we can challenge our belief to see whether we want to change it, or we may feel that we need a particular person's friendship, and that we can't get along without it. This is an irrational belief. It is true we need friendship, but we don't absolutely need the friendship of any one individual. We can receive support from several persons and not just one. If we believe we need friendship from one individual only, then we become depressed if that individual dies, or if the person refuses friendship. This is an irrational belief that must be challenged. Behind our feelings are beliefs, and it's profitable for us to be aware of the beliefs or assumptions we have accumulated over the years in order to be more effective pastoral persons.[15]

Footnotes

[1] Thomas A. Kane, *The Healing Touch of Affirmation*, Affirmation Books, Whitinsville, MA, 1976, p. 80.

[2] Molly Young Brown, *Growing Whole*, Harper Collins, New York, NY, 1993, pp. 11 & 12.

[3] Everett L. Shostrom, *Man The Manipulator*, Bantam Books, New York, NY, 1968, pp. 40-43.

[4] Carl Rogers, "The Place of Feelings and Emotions," *Mental Health Info-Pak Cassette Series*, Tape 2, Instructional Dynamics Incorporated, Chicago, IL.

[5] John Powell, *Why Am I Afraid To Tell You Who I Am?*, Argus Communications, Chicago, IL, 1969, pp. 54-62.

[6] John Powell, *The Secret of Staying in Love*, Argus Communications, Niles, IL, 1974, pp. 80-81.

[7] Carolyn Foster, *The Family Patterns Workbook*, Putnam Publishing Co., New York, NY, 1993, pp. 127-133.

[8] Bernard J. Bush, *Intimacy: Issues of Emotional Living in an Age of Stress for Clergy and Religious*, Affirmation Books, Whitinsville, MA, 1978, pp. 48-51.

[9] Fran Ferder, *Words Made Flesh*, Ave Maria Press, Notre Dame, IN, 1986, pp. 170-176.

[10] John Powell, *Why Am I Afraid To Tell You Who I Am?*, *op. cit.*, pp. 79-84.

[11] Molly Young Brown, *op. cit.*, pp. 98 & 99.

[12] John Powell, *Why Am I Afraid To Tell You Who I Am?*, *op. cit.*, pp. 65-77.

[13] Thomas A. Kane, *op. cit.*, p. 79.

[14] Willard Gaylin, *Feelings — Our Vital Signs*, Harper & Row, New York, NY, 1979, p. 39.

[15] John J. Malecki and Susanne Breckel, *Sexuality: The Celibate's Response*, National Assembly of Religious Brothers, Tape 3, Passionist Broadcasting, West Springfield, MA, 1978.

CHAPTER FIVE

AUTHORITY

S EVERAL YEARS AGO AFTER THE LOCAL bishop blessed a new church, the clergy participating in the blessing were invited to dinner in the undercroft of the church. As usually happens when priests gather, small groups formed and camaraderie was quickly established. However, as the bishop entered the undercroft, the atmosphere quickly changed. The priests' voices became noticeably softer, and there was an immediate movement to the various tables to prepare to eat. The pastor escorted the bishop to the head table, but no one chose to sit with them. So the bishop pleaded with some of his priests to join him for the meal. Reluctantly, a few slowly moved forward until the head table was filled. These priests did not want to sit with their bishop because they feared his scrutiny. They were uncomfortable with him. There was a certain distance between the bishop and his priests; there was no peer relationship, no real rapport, no true friendship between them.

Feelings Toward Authority

Underlying these feelings of uncomfortableness with a person in authority are feelings of fear because the boss has power over us. She/he can transfer us from one position to another, can change our whole life by moving us from a city and people we love to a city 150 miles away where we know no one. Another reason for fearing authority is our perception that these persons in authority are only present to criticize us. Possibly this feeling exists because in the past affirmation came from superiors very infrequently and criticism very often. Even many of our parents were not instructed how to affirm us as human beings, but rather how to correct and mold us to become obedient children.

Associated with these feelings of fear are those of suspicion. Some of us are constantly on guard for fear the boss will take advantage of us. He might give us more than our share of the work, might take a day off and leave hospital calls for us to handle, might go to a banquet or lunch and eat prime rib while we eat hamburger. The superior attends workshops in Florida and California while we are limited to those within 300 miles. Beneath this kind of suspicion is the idea that people in power always get the best by "using" their subordinates, resulting in an attitude of "we'd better look out for ourselves." One young priest who had this attitude always noted bitterly when his pastor got his haircut and took care of his personal banking needs on a day the pastor was supposed to be working. Naturally associated with these feelings of suspicion are feelings of anger toward authority.

Coping With These Feelings

When we are uncomfortable in the presence of authority figures, oftentimes we either fight or flee them. This is a very normal reaction. If we observe the major coping behaviors of subhuman groups in which there is conflict between animals of the same species, we usually observe two patterns, the flight or fight response on the part of one of them. Both fighting and running away are very efficient ways for animals to deal with each other. These methods of coping seem to be almost automatic responses with great survival success in the lower animals. We fight and run from each other as human beings too, although this is not always done freely and openly. Most often we do it in ways that are disguised from each other. In spite of the fact that we have flight and fight in common with the lower animals, what distinguishes us from them is our verbal and problem-solving brain that has given us great superiority over the animals.[1]

Sometimes we flee authority figures by moving many miles from them. A priest happily takes a parish some distance from the main city in the diocese to escape the possible scrutiny of his bishop. A woman lay minister gladly offers to visit the shut-ins of the parish to avoid meeting frequently with the pastor as the religious education director does. We seldom attend social gatherings and meetings when we know the superior will be present, unless we feel it's "a must." When we do attend, we try our best to avoid the person in authority, sitting far away from him.

Some other people react by constantly fighting with authority. Possibly in every group there are one or two people who criticize every guideline the bishop or religious superior gives. These people are rebelling in general. They balk against religious and civil authority with equal venom. They join every march which attacks an authority figure. In their immaturity, these persons rebel for the sake of rebelling and in this way are ventilating some of their pent-up hostility toward authority in general, like the high school student who expressed hostility toward authority by throwing a pie in the face of a teacher. Most often instead of engaging in a direct and constructive interchange, they say of a person in authority, "She should mind her own business." Or perhaps they use a more modern form of criticism, "She doesn't practice collegiality." Another version of this modern argument is, "It's contrary to Vatican II because there is no shared decision-making taking place."

A unique example of fleeing from authority occurred in an interpersonal group which I recently led. There were seven members and we were discussing the date of our next session, which had to be changed because of a holiday. One member said she could not make it on Wednesday and I said Tuesday was bad for me. Another member immediately urged the group to meet on Tues-

day. This member made this suggestion because he feared authority as he said earlier, "I don't like authority because they often take
advantage of you. They boss you around too much." As the leader
of the group, I represented authority for him and so he was eager
to have a session without me, to distance himself from me. At the
same time, he seemed to be saying that the group didn't need any
"authority," that in his life things would be better without one.

A danger that results from distancing ourselves from superiors is the fact that we easily become isolated. We become our own
authorities since we don't interact with persons in authority or even
our peers. No one ever confronts us about our decisions. We become a law unto ourselves, and no one ever challenges us because
we clearly are "the boss." When we meet infrequently with superiors, they sense our discomfort, insecurity, and fear, and since they
don't know how to handle that, they become uncomfortable. As a
result, they don't seek us out, but rather allow us to maintain our
distance from them and continue our non-constructive behavior.[2]

Another way of reacting to authority besides flight and fight
is that of total submission. In early September of my first year of
philosophy, the Archbishop ordered us to pray the Litany of the
Saints every day after Mass for rain so that the crops would be plen-
tiful. Unfortunately, the drought that started in August continued
throughout September. We kept on praying the litany daily until
the middle of October when the Archbishop was finally asked if we
could stop doing so. Even though I am not a farmer, I don't think
rain in October would benefit the fall harvest after two rainless
months. However, this decision could not be made on our own,
but needed to come from the Archbishop. This kind of excessive
dependence discourages claiming our own authority. It encouraged
us to be completely obedient, conforming to every utterance that
comes forth from any person in authority. It urged us to be extremely
dependent, looking to authority for solutions to every problem. As
a result, we thought very little on our own and always asked superiors many questions to avoid accepting responsibility for our own
decisions. We never disagreed with authority, nor shared any of our

own real feelings or opinions, but rather adopted their opinions as our own. This reminds me of the old doggerel which expresses more truth than we perhaps would like to admit:

> To the bishop as he mounted
> for the first time to his throne
> bent the princely Consecrator
> with his confidential tone:
> "Two things only in this office
> merit certainty, forsooth:
> Nevermore to pay for dinner
> Nevermore to hear the truth."

This attitude is illustrated more clearly by referring to Lawrence Kohlberg's "Stages of Moral Development." His first stage is entitled punishment and obedience because it emphasizes avoiding punishment through unquestioning deference to those in power. His second stage is best explained by the phrase, "You scratch my back and I'll scratch yours." At this time persons are interested mainly in satisfying their own needs and occasionally the needs of others. Good intentions become important in the third stage in which good behavior is described as trying to please or help others. It's also important to earn approval by being "nice."[3]

When persons have successfully completed all three of these stages, then they enter the fourth stage which is total submission to authority as was described earlier. When people are in this stage, there is a tremendous emphasis on law. At this point there is an orientation toward authority, fixed rules, maintaining order in society, and doing one's duty. Persons at this stage fear deviating from rules because that might lead to social chaos. Here they view their obligation to obey the law as more important than their obligations to their friends and groups. They sympathize with well-intentioned people who break the law, but this sympathy is overridden by their concern for keeping the social order which demands a strict adherence to rules and authority. There is no room for any autonomy in judgment, no possibility of using their own minds to decide what is right and wrong. They rely totally upon law and give blind obedience to it.[4]

In this phase of moral development, people tend to interpret the Bible very strictly and frequently refer to God as a lawgiver rather than as a loving and merciful Father. In this strict interpretation of the Bible, they demand perfection of themselves in order to be saved and do the same for others. In reading God's word they emphasize those passages where God punishes people for their lack of obedience and other passages where he rewards people for adherence to the law. Damnation is frequently mentioned.

This type of total submission to authority recalls the Watergate Trial, when defendants stated they did not intend to violate any laws, but were only doing what they were told to do by their superiors. During the trial, the judge made it clear that people are not virtuous who obey commands blindly, but insisted that subordinates reflect on the commands given to them to make sure they are ethical and within the competence of those issuing them. The reaction of the general public indicated that they agreed with this, and that it is not sufficient for a person to be well-intentioned.

Sometimes this total submission expresses itself in a pastoral care program when students constantly quote their supervisor rather than express any of their own ideas. At other times it is displayed by insecure students who frequently praise their supervisor, with the hope that this will win the acceptance of the supervisor which is needed badly to bolster a poor self-image. One religious woman interacted with me in that manner telling me, "You have great insight. You amaze me how much you know what's going on in a group. You really present interesting lectures too. I'm never bored. I put your ideas into practice and they always work with the patients too. You're simply amazing." I enjoyed the compliments but, at the same time, realized that they were coming from her need for my acceptance.

Source of our Attitudes and Feelings

In order to mature in our relationships with authority, it is necessary to look at authority openly to consider how we acquired our present attitudes. A good place to begin is to reflect on our attitude toward our parents. While growing up, were we frequently threatened with punishment? Threatened to be sent to bed without our supper if we did not obey immediately? Threatened constantly of being deprived of new clothes or our privileges if we came home fifteen minutes after the curfew? Possibly some of us were reared in an atmosphere where we were frequently told, "Children should be seen and not heard." We were constantly reminded to respect our parents, a respect that caused fear and distance from them. In this atmosphere, no doubt there were times when we became not only fearful of our parents, but angry with them because they demanded perfection of us. Naturally, we could not measure up to their scrupulous demands and consequently did not feel cherished, loved and valued.

On the other hand, maybe we were blessed to grow up in a home where we were often affirmed as a human being. We were loved and accepted just for being who we are, without any obligation to produce in order to gain approval. We were reared in a warm, loving atmosphere where our parents displayed their affection for us with many hugs and kisses, yet still grew up with an understanding of the meaning of "no." Such a person was Pope John XXIII. Because of the affirmation he received as a child, he was constantly affirming people in his life. Whether it was in personal contact or on television, young and old, Catholics and non-Catholics, all over the world were touched by Pope John's affirmation.

An example of his ability to affirm people occurred when he visited the inmates of Regina Coeli prison in Rome under a blue, cloudless sky. In his address to the prisoners, he expressed his pleasure at the opportunity of visiting them and recalled for them that one of his cousins had once served a term in prison. He concluded his talk, "I have come. You have seen. I have looked into your eyes.

I have placed my heart alongside your heart." After his formal greeting, a few prisoners were permitted to approach him and kiss his ring. One of them, a murderer, looked at him with sad eyes and asked, "Are those words of hope you have given me for such a great sinner as I am?" In response, Pope John bent over the convict and embraced him.[5]

A beautiful example of an affirming person in my own life was Joe Emmanuel, a professor of counseling at Wright State University. I was one of eight participants in a growth group he was leading. At the beginning of each session, he asked us how we were working on our goals for personal growth. Because of the atmosphere of affirmation that he created, people were less hesitant to share their failures. Initially he affirmed persons in their struggles to grow, but after a short time the members supported one another, following his example. In other words, he was a catalyst in forming an accepting, affirming group of people who never knew each other before the group began.

Next, it is profitable to evaluate our attitude toward God as an authority person. How do we view God? Are we fearful of God because we look upon him as a just judge, a lawgiver, one who rewards the good and punishes the evil? Do we look upon ourselves as being nothing in his presence, as absolutely worthless? Another attitude toward God is feeling comfortable in his presence because he is a forgiving, loving Father/Mother who many times forgave the Jewish people when they turned their backs on him. He is a person who continually seems to give people another chance to love him, a person like Hosea who loves even an adulterous wife. Associated with this concept of God is the idea that God has given us certain talents and gifts. He has blessed us with certain skills which he expects us to use. God loves us and that's why he gifted us.

Probably, our feelings toward our dad and our God are similar. After all, both of them are authority figures whom we call "father." It's beneficial for us to reexamine these attitudes to see if we would like to change any of them. If we are uncomfortable being with authority persons, we might want to rid ourselves of fear toward them, rid ourselves of any "tapes" that demand perfection of us, and consider whether we would like to claim peer status with them as fellow adults.

Some women have their own unique struggles with authority because their mothers viewed themselves as inferior to men, and they conveyed this message to their daughters. Their mothers perceived themselves as having the role of pleasing and charming men, and passed on this notion of "unequality" to their daughters. As a result of these negative messages over the years, women and other disempowered groups tend to feel like frauds when their feelings reflect internalized values that tell them that women don't belong in spheres of authority.[6] When women feel hesitant, apologetic, silenced, and self-doubting, it may reflect their refusal to internalize the idea that they have a right to power. One woman medical doctor illustrated this clearly. When she would go to the coffee shop in the hospital, she was reluctant to identify herself as an M.D. and further refused to accept the praise that periodically she rightly deserved because of her outstanding work.[7]

Associated with this source of our feelings toward authority is our self-image. Some people feel comfortable in the presence of authority figures, or fear them because they are insecure persons and so give them more authority over them than they actually have. These persons attribute perfection to superiors and worthlessness to themselves. Those who feel this way might be classified as "pleasers" because they are constantly striving to gratify other people, to conform their lives at the expense of self-determination. "Pleasers" base their lives on being accepted and approved by others, especially those in authority, and suffer guilt feelings when they fail to satisfy them. They consider the evaluations of others as the measuring rod of their self-worth, regardless of who they are or how many talents they possess, regardless of what accomplishments they have attained. Life is meaningless for them unless people approve of them. However, when others accept them, that approval is often short-lived because they find it difficult to accept and sometimes, even impossible to believe. They tend to doubt the sincerity of compliments and constantly seek more signs of approval.[8]

One lady who was studying in graduate school for her doctorate in psychology was such a person. She was blessed with good intellect, an attractive personality, and a high degree of natural beauty. However, her father, a farmer, thought that women ought to go to high school, get married, have children, and take care of the home. Because of his strong emphasis on that role for women, he never affirmed her as intelligent or as attractive in personality or appearance. So she didn't believe in her own worth. Finally, one day in a group sensitivity session, a member became very angry at her, saying, "I am damned tired of you rejecting my compliments. I feel that you are intelligent, that you are easy to get along with and you reject these statements. In effect, you are saying that I am stupid or lying and I don't like either implication." This was a turning point in this young lady's life, because from this time on she realized how much authority she allowed her father to have over her and how difficult it was for her to accept compliments. If we pastoral care persons are going to function effectively, we must practice what is mentioned in the book *If You Meet the Buddha on the Road Kill Him*. The book points out that all of us are pilgrims, all of us are equal, all of us have our own talents and insights, and no one should be placed on a pedestal, as far superior to us. In other words, the author is urging us to claim our own authority and our own giftedness.[9]

Another aspect of "pleasers" is that their lives are like a yoyo, going up and down depending on how many compliments they receive. Naturally, if someone offers criticism, that causes them to become depressed for some period of time. Thus, they are like putty in the hands of other people, extremely dependent upon them for support.

Those who possess poor self-images can improve them by engaging in exercises to build self-esteem, to acquire the skill of self-affirmation, and to monitor negative thinking.[10] David Burns has written a book of exercises to build self-esteem. He outlines ten steps toward self-acceptance and self-esteem. Many people have found his suggestions helpful.[11] Melody Beattie has a slightly different approach. She writes of "having a love affair with yourself" and supports her idea by quoting William Shakespeare, "This above all to thine own self be true, and it must follow, as the night the day, thou canst not then be false to any man." Her main thesis is that we need to honor ourselves.[12]

Ingrid Trobisch approaches enhancing our self-esteem in a different manner. She devotes a chapter to "Accepting God's Acceptance of Us" in her book *The Confident Woman*. Here she uses the Bible and prayer as a means to this end, giving herself the freedom to adjust the gender of the Scriptures. "Blessed is the woman who trusts in the Lord, whose hope is the Lord. She is like a tree planted beside the waters that stretches out its roots to the stream" (Jr 17:7-8).[13]

Authority and Our Response

Some people have an idealistic way of looking at things, and so fantasize about a world in which there is no authority, in which there is absolute freedom for everyone. This is pure fantasy because throughout our lives there are going to be persons in authority to whom we must report; everyone is responsible to someone; everyone has a boss. This is a fact of life. Even the president of our nation reports to Congress and is not totally free.

As human beings, God is an authority in our lives. Since he is our Creator, he has a right to establish commandments for us; he has a right to tell us how to live through the teachings and example of Jesus Christ in the gospels. As pastoral persons, an obvious authority is the Church and its leader, the Pope, for Roman Catholics. His encyclicals and decrees as well as those of his offices in Rome demand our respect. Next, we have the bishop of our diocese or the superintendent of our district. For many of us, there is a pastor or hospital president to whom we report. Finally, some of us have church councils and commissions which demand our deference. In addition to these persons and commissions invested with authority, all of us have friends who have some authority over us.

A friend is someone whom we trust, someone whose opinions are worthy of our consideration. We freely give that person some authority over us and in turn have some authority over him/her. There is a certain interdependence between us.

Recognizing that all of us are responsible to someone and report to some authority (superior), we now have the choice of responding or reacting to that person. We can react to authority with uncomfortableness, fear, anger, a desire to escape, etc., or we can choose to respond by giving it an appropriate place in our lives. In responding to authority, we recognize that it does exist, but it has limits. In responding to authority, we know that authority does not have the power to control our whole lives, nor power to destroy us; however, it has power over certain aspects of our lives. Thus, persons in authority might demand that we change our lifestyle to some extent. We might be required to compromise some of our patterns of behavior or methods of functioning in a work situation. This compromise results, though, from an open and direct interaction with persons in authority where we feel comfortable enough to share our opinions and feelings, and in turn feel comfortable enough to listen to the feelings and opinions of our boss.

In other words, we feel at ease with persons in authority. We are comfortable with God because we view God as a kind, merciful being who loves us so much that he made us to his own image and likeness. We regard God as a kindly Father and/or Mother who is interested in us and our welfare. We look upon God as one who values us so much that he gave each of us talents and gifts, and the greatest of all gifts, his own Son, Jesus.

As mature individuals, we look upon human persons in authority not as our masters, but rather as persons who are trying to serve us. We regard the Pope as the "servant of servants" rather than as a majestic superior to whom we must offer homage. We look upon superiors as those who assist in our growth, as those who assist us in fulfilling the will of God, rather than as persons who have power over us. In the true sense of the word "authority" which has its roots in the word "author," the pastor or administrator is a developer, an enabler. A person in authority is like the author of a book, an originator, a designer, one who develops and brings the hidden reality into existence. Persons with structured positions of authority need to meditate often upon this concept so that they never use their authority as "power over people." An authority, like Jesus Christ, is one who enables, develops, helps design the possibility for the actualization of the potential of the persons entrusted to his care.

In psychological terms, the purpose of authority is the ultimate development of self-direction and self-regulation so that an individual may live a resourceful and abundant life. The purpose of authority is not to control other people but rather to lessen control on others. Many individuals view authority as discipline which is interpreted as punishment or severe arbitrary restrictions imposed in order to punish or to teach someone a lesson. This notion is so common that the role of legitimate authority in leading the person towards self-regulation and self-direction is often ignored or repudiated when it is rightfully offered.[14]

Claiming Our Own Authority

It is important to recognize our own authority too. Part of the growth process in becoming effective pastoral persons is to claim our own authority. This means claiming rights that are ours as persons, claiming our Bill of Rights, the right to be treated with respect, the right to be listened to and taken seriously, the right to ask for what we want, the right to ask for information from other professionals, the right to have and express our own feelings and opinions, the right to choose not to assert ourselves, and the right to make mistakes.

When clergy fail to claim their authority, that affects their ministry. As chaplains introduce themselves to patients in a hospital, some state clearly their authority: "I'm Mary Brown, the chaplain of the unit." Others who are unsure of themselves are very meek in their introduction: "I'm Mary and I dropped by to see you," or "I'm Mike Thoms, one of the students here in the chaplaincy program." In these last two examples, the persons did not assume their authority as chaplain of the floor.

Some of us indicate our comfortableness with ourselves by allowing the patient to take the conversation wherever she/he wishes, while others are anxious and display it by a need to control the conversation. They ask very direct questions frequently and thereby control the topics of the conversation. Their anxiety is further indicated by their need to speak all the time and never to permit brief silences which might allow the patient to reflect on what was said, or to introduce a significant topic of their own.

It happens sometimes that we are too quick to refer people to other professionals. We refer to the head chaplain, the social worker or the nurse instead of ministering to the person ourselves. A patient asks a theological question, and immediately we feel our inadequacy in the matter and call for a theologian. A patient expresses feelings of depression, and we quickly excuse ourselves to call for a psychologist or social worker to help with the patient. Often upset people speak to us about these matters because they like us and hope we will assist them, and not immediately refer them to someone else. If we do decide to refer, then this is done with the person's knowledge and with the realization that someone more skilled than ourselves is needed.

Those of us who fail to claim our authority as professional chaplains, also tend to avoid certain topics. If the patient introduces the possibility of his dying, we might strive to reduce our uneasiness by switching the subject to a safe topic, such as the weather. However, when our identity and authority is certain, we are willing to walk through the valley of death with them and at their pace, nor ours.

Finally when we claim our own authority in visiting the sick, we are aware of the valuable contribution we are making to their welfare. When a doctor or nurse interrupts our conversation without even excusing themselves, we let them know we are also professionals with specific skills to employ for the patient's benefit. This is often very difficult and a real test of our own authority, because we tend in our culture to be overawed by the medical profession. There is the added difficulty in deciding an appropriate place to communicate to the medical person our displeasure at such discourtesy. One time when a doctor did this to me, I interrupted his conversation with the patient to introduce myself so that he knew I existed. Other times I have waited for the doctor outside the patient's room to convey my hurt feeling. Each of us must choose for ourselves how to respond, but it is important to claim our own authority in some manner.

If without consulting us our pastor or administrator makes a decision which affects us, this presents another opportunity to claim our rights as persons. As a person, we have a right to be consulted before such a decision is made. Most leaders are happy to know that they have moved too fast and neglected to seek consultation appropriately.

Authority and Freedom

Naturally, there is tension between the authority of pastors or the chief chaplain and the freedom of other members of the pastoral team. Sometimes the leaders think that others are exercising too much freedom, while at other times the pastoral people doing the field work think their leaders are abusing their authority by setting down too many rules. However, authority and liberty are twin sisters who cannot live without each other, and they need not be in conflict. After all, as we stated earlier, the function of authority is to guide others to their proper destiny. Authority in some persons is for liberty in others. So authority is harmonious with individual freedom; they are complementary to one another, and not opposed.[15]

However, in reality there are times when struggles exist between them. Part of this is due to the fact that we are dealing with human beings. Another is that there is a period of adjustment going on at the present time, with more freedom being given individuals than ever before. Our culture and the teachings of the Second Vatican Council are urging this. Presently there is a tendency to moderate the influence of external law and of authority in general, and to increase personal responsibility. It is beneficial to remember though, that freedom is not license, nor the absence of all restraints, but rather the ability to do what one feels God is calling one to do. In the words of Pope Paul VI:

> ... at the same time, we must be conscious of the fact that our Christian liberty does not remove us from the law of God in the ultimate demands it makes on us in the realms of human wisdom, of evangelical spirit, of self control, of penance, and of obedience to the communitarian order proper to an ecclesial society. Christian liberty is not charismatic in the arbitrary sense that is claimed for us by some prophets of our time: St. Peter the Apostle teaches us to act as free men — not as men who make of liberty a camouflage for their malice, but as servants of God (1 P 2:16).[16]

Freedom provides the opportunity to choose, to select options. It includes the possibility of making mistakes, to say that we don't know the answer to that question. Freedom is to be real, to share ourselves with others, our strengths, our weaknesses even, with superiors. Freedom means, with the help of God, to establish our own standards to measure ourselves by, rather than to adopt standards that are imposed by others. It means to follow our own informed consciences. It means to experience the love of others for one's self, to give love to others. Finally it means to value one's self as having worth.

To achieve an appropriate balance between authority and freedom it may be profitable to look at St. Paul's epistles where he stresses the importance of law and at the same time freedom of the sons and daughters of God, freedom of the spirit. Another helpful source to assist in achieving this balance may be assertive training groups which encourage self-expression, but with some concern for other persons. The first tenet of many of these training groups is that we respect ourselves and others. This respect is shown by standing up for ourselves — expressing our thoughts, feelings and preferences and at the same time being mindful of the rights and feelings of the other person. The second tenet urges us to be aware that life cannot be lived without hurting people from time to time. It's important for us to understand that other people are not so fragile that they will be crushed forever by something we do or say. We need to trust that other people have a certain elasticity about them to bounce back from a hurt they might receive. Besides, if we live fearing we might hurt someone, then we will be paralyzed and unable to do anything. The third premise is that sacrificing integrity and denying our own needs harms personal and community relationships which are built only on trust and openness. As a result, we keep our relatives and friends at arm's length and force them to guess how they might assist us. Often too, they know something has upset us and they waste a lot of time and energy trying to figure out what it was they said or did that caused it. When we share our needs and feelings openly with others, it is much more loving. The final belief is that sacrificing our own rights and needs teaches others to take advantage of us. On the other hand, when we tell others how they affect us, this gives them a chance to change and grow in their relationship to us and probably to other people as well.[17]

Conclusion

There are four possible responses to authority by pastoral care persons. First, in our relationship to authority we can be very passive, submitting ourselves totally to persons in authority. This means that we never express our feelings, thoughts or preferences. We limit ourselves to occasional hints at them and often deny them. We make requests indirectly, apologetically, and even self-effacingly. Our body language says, "Pardon me for living." Consequently, we violate our own rights as human beings. Second, we respond to authority aggressively, demanding our rights, forcing certain things to take place. With this attitude we stand up for our rights, but we have no concern for the rights of others. We want our own way no matter what we have to do to get it. We humiliate or demean others in order to get what we want. Third, we respond to authority in a passive-aggressive manner. We get what we want when we want it, but we attain our goal in an indirect way. We are dishonest, make others feel guilty, and use sarcasm. We do not relate to our immediate superior, but rather go to the personnel director or the bishop to obtain our goal. At times we put on the "poor me" attitude, and at other times give people the silent treatment. We are a master at manipulation to attain our goal.

Finally, as mature Christians, we are assertive in our behavior expressing our thoughts, feelings and preferences clearly, and leaving the other person to respond or not. Here open communication is practiced. We respect ourselves and we respect other people. We stand up for our own rights, but we do not violate the rights of others. This requires honesty, humility, and charity. It is risky. This kind of assertive behavior does not guarantee success in our relationships with authority and other people, but it certainly does increase the odds of relating effectively with them.

Footnotes

[1] Manuel J. Smith, *When I Say No, I Feel Guilty*, Bantam Books, Inc., New York, NY, 1975, p. 5.

[2] James F. Campbell, "Priests, Authority and Growth," *Pastoral Life*, June, 1977, p. 34.

[3] Ronald Duska and Mariellen Whelan, *Moral Development: A Guide to Piaget and Kohlberg*, Paulist Press, New York, NY, 1975, pp. 45-47.

[4] Ronald Duska and Mariellen Whelan, *op. cit.*, pp. 64-66.

[5] Conrad W. Baars, *Born Only Once*, Franciscan Herald Press, Chicago, IL, 1975, pp. 45-46.

[6] Nancy Tuana, *The Less Noble Sex*, Indiana University Press, Bloomington, IN, 1993, p. 59.

[7] Harriet Goldhor-Lerner, *The Dance of Deception*, Harper Collins, New York, NY, 1993, pp. 74-77.

[8] Joseph L. Hart, "Perils of the Pleasers," *Loneliness*, edited by James P. Madden, Affirmation Books, Whitinsville, MA, 1977, pp. 45-50.

[9] Sheldon B. Kopp, *If You Meet The Buddha On The Road Kill Him*, Bantam Books, Inc., New York, NY, 1976, p. 19.

[10] Mary McConnell, *Still Dancing*, Harbinger House, New York, NY, 1990, pp. 96-98.

[11] David A. Burns, *Ten Days to Self-Esteem*, Quill/William Morrow, New York, NY, 1993, pp. 122-140.

[12] Melody Beattie, *Co-Dependent No More*, Harper/Hazeldon, San Francisco, CA, 1987, pp. 109-131.

[13] Ingrid Trobisch, *The Confident Woman*, Harper Publishing, San Francisco, CA, 1993, pp. 20-22.

[14] James J. Rue and Louise Shanhan, *Daddy's Girl, Mama's Boy*, The Bobbs-Merrill Company, Inc., Indianapolis, IN, 1978, pp. 31-33.

[15] Donald DeMarco, "The Foundation of Morality and the Function of Authority," *Review for Religious*, September, 1978, p. 704.

[16] Pope Paul VI, "Allocution of Pope Paul VI," Wednesday, July 9, 1979.

[17] Robert E. Alberti and Michael L. Emmons, *Your Perfect Right*, Impact Publishers, San Luis Obispo, CA, 1978, pp. 27-28.

CHAPTER SIX

ANGER

B EING IN THE PRESENCE OF A HUSBAND and wife who are in a
heated argument is probably more embarrassing to us and
to them than if we inadvertently discovered them in a passionate embrace. That's because we have been taught it's not proper
to display anger. How did we come to regard anger as such an objectionable emotion? We were conditioned to have this attitude
through our parental training, our religious education, and our modeling of the significant adults in our lives.

Our conditioning began in our early childhood. As toddlers,
we vented our anger through crying; later as small children, we
resorted to temper tantrums which may have included kicking and
biting. Our parents, no doubt, punished us for such behavior, and
we received the message that anger is bad. As children, too, we
sometimes teased or fought with our sister and were told, "That's
your sister, don't hit her; you're supposed to love her instead of
hitting her." Again we picked up the message that anger is bad.
Religion teachers often emphasized the many things parents were
doing for us as children and so urged us always to be loving and
grateful to them. The underlying message was that we could never
be angry with them; there was no mention of the possibility of loving them and being angry with them at the same time.

Another important factor in our attitude toward anger was our
modeling of our parents when they became angry. How did they
handle their anger? We knew them well enough to know that cer-

tain things we did or the neighbors did, made them mad. We watched what they did with their anger. If they became enraged, we wanted to hide because of our fear of them, and at the same time we became fearful of the emotion of anger. If they "sat on" their anger, then we learned that repression was the way to handle anger.[1]

Our culture has generally made it more difficult for women to deal with anger then men because of the assumption that the ingredients of women are sugar and spice. This means women's role is to be nurturers, peacemakers and steadiers of the rocked boat. It is their job to please, protect and placate. In addition, the taboos in our society against women feeling and expressing anger are so powerful that it is difficult for them to even know they are angry. It is interesting how our culture approves of angry men who are striving to right a wrong. However, when women express their anger, men sometimes judge them as unladylike, witches, hags, or dismiss them as irrational or over-emotional. This seems to be especially true when women are angry at men.[2]

Why do we become angry? Our anger may be telling us that we are hurting, that a basic right is being violated or a basic need is not being met. Anger may be a message that some beliefs, values, or hopes are being compromised in a relationship. Anger may be a signal that the demands at work or at home are too great, are more than we can reasonably do. Many times we become angry because our expectations are not being met.

When dictators and governments in Third World countries prevent the satisfaction of basic needs for large numbers of people, the citizens become angry. The people of Latin America participate in revolutions periodically because they are poor and hungry. They have no land and no power. They are sick and have no medicine. They live in constant fear of abduction and torture. Their basic survival needs are threatened. They hope a new government will make things better for them. It is not surprising that the rate of violent crimes is highest in those parts of the city where poverty is the greatest. Often these people are caught in a cycle of poverty and hopelessness, and express it in violent crimes.[3]

Our difficulties in dealing with the emotion of anger were increased when we were taught as youngsters that anger was sinful. When we grew older, we were taught that there were times when it was permissible to get angry, but there had to be justifiable reasons, such as those which Jesus had when he drove the money changers out of the Temple with a whip. This, however, didn't allow us many opportunities to become angry without sinning.

Actually, of course, there were many other times in the Bible when Jesus became angry. He was angry with the scribes and Pharisees on a number of occasions, and once was so angry he called them whited sepulchers. Several times he was angry with his apostles because they could not understand that he had to suffer and die before entering into his glory, even though he spoke clearly of a spiritual kingdom. Other times, he became angry with them because they were arguing about who was going to be the greatest in his kingdom. An additional factor in our education concerning anger is that religious leaders held up the "meek Jesus" during his sufferings as the model to imitate. Pastoral care persons today are challenged to present the "total Jesus" as a model worthy of imitation, that is, Jesus who expressed not only his love and acceptance of the limitations of others, but his anger and frustration as well.

Sharing Our Anger

So our home and religious training in most cases instilled in us an attitude that makes us uncomfortable when we experience our anger, and especially uncomfortable when the anger is directed to our mother, father, good friend, spouse, or religious superior. An additional reason for our uneasiness is the fear that anger destroys relationships.

As persons who "don't make waves," we fear anger kills the love we have for another and then ask ourselves how we could possibly live without love. Anger naturally makes waves and does kill this kind of irrational love that depends on displaying 100% harmony. In reality, of course, this isn't love at all but a kind of neurotic dependency which is confused with love. So, anger doesn't destroy healthy relationships, nor does it kill people. Rather, denying anger can result in the killing of relationships and people too. Becoming angry and sharing angry feelings strengthens true love and actually affirms a relationship. A novice director, for example, shared her anger with a young nun for coming late for an appointment. At this, the novice responded with some anger, telling her the circumstances causing her tardiness. Once their anger was shared with the reasons for it, both felt closer to one another realizing that in their open relationship it's O.K. to become angry with each other. Thus, it isn't anger that kills, but those people who are frequently divorced from all their feelings and unaware of their rage.[4]

Another aspect of the problem is dealing with ambivalent feelings, feelings of love and anger or hate toward the same person. The old childhood messages of exclusiveness remain: we either feel love or anger, but not both simultaneously. As a result, we say to ourselves, "I love my friend, I want him to be my friend always, so how can I be angry with him?" We are confused by these ambivalent feelings, not believing they are possible. In reality though, hate and love are not mutually exclusive, and it is possible to love a friend and to be angry when he comes half an hour late for our golf outing. It's important to make anger serve love by integrating the two of them. This is done when we share our anger by being able to fight with those whom we love. However, this fighting occurs in such a manner that there is respect for each other's vulnerable spots, so that there is no hitting below the belt which causes the other person to feel overwhelmed. This means channeling our angry feelings so that they are released in a constructive way.[5]

Another aspect is the confusion that often surrounds the meaning of anger. Today there are a number of "anger workshops" and "self-assertion workshops" as if they are the same. Anger and self-assertion, however, are different. *Webster's New Collegiate Dictionary* defines anger as "emotional excitement induced by intense displeasure." This definition describes a reaction, but it carries with it no judgments or predictions of loss of control. It simply identifies a reaction to intense displeasure. Fury, wrath, and rage describe a loss of control, accompanied by destruction or pain. So anger workshops deal with identifying and channeling intense displeasure. Self-assertion workshops, on the other hand, enable shy people to feel free to stand up for their own rights. Another word confused with anger is aggression which is sometimes associated with destruction. This causes us to reject anger as unacceptable with our image of a good Christian. Usually though, destruction and loss of control result from anger that is unidentified.

Once we realize that anger is nothing but intense displeasure, then we are more readily able to own our anger. For example, Mary had made plans to take a vacation for three months and had finalized all the arrangements when the boss informs her that her request for the time off has been cancelled; Pam is driving along the road at the speed limit and somebody behind her keeps blowing the horn, commanding her to go faster; a pastoral staff plans several hours for a meaningful reconciliation rite for the whole parish and then only a handful of people show up for the service. These incidents and many others, which are as common as rain and sunshine, are occasions to become angry. It's healthy to allow ourselves to own the anger, realizing this is not something controllable to a large extent, but rather is part of human nature. These feelings of anger are similar to feelings of a sexual nature. They are part and parcel of being a human being.

Constructive Use of Angry Feelings

From experience it is evident we can't rid ourselves of these angry feelings by walking them away, by talking them away, by drinking them away, by smoking them away, nor by sleeping them away. So as pastoral persons we need to learn how to deal with them constructively in our lives and to assist others to do the same. In handling all feelings effectively, and in particular angry feelings, it is essential to experience the feelings. After identifying them, as mature adults we decide how to express them, if we wish to express them at all. As rational beings, the intellect comes into play in determining how to communicate our feelings. It is our choice as Christians. The question is not whether we become angry or not, but rather how and when to share our feelings. Thus in dealing with anger effectively, there are three steps: identifying the feelings of anger, accepting these feelings as being part of humanity, and then deciding the manner of expressing them, if that is our choice. The important thing is knowing and accepting angry feelings because this in itself mitigates against collecting and storing anger. Combining real acceptance of angry feelings without any judgment of them, along with the ability to express the anger in a constructive way, enables us to grow as mature persons.

The idea of sharing our anger is not something that takes a long time to decide, nor is delaying the expression of anger always the most effective manner of dealing with it. Rather the opposite is often true. It's best to share the anger at the time it occurs. The longer we wait, the less effective the message is, although sometimes circumstances dictate a delay or non-sharing of our anger. When there is a time lapse between the feelings of anger and the expression, then it is more difficult for the other person to accurately recall the circumstances surrounding the incident and the strength of the message is dissipated.[6] When a chaplain was fired from her position at a hospital for a reason that seemed inadequate to her, it was far better that she shared her anger before leaving the hospital, rather than carrying her belongings as well as her pent-up anger home with her.

Realizing that anger is an important aspect of personality, it is easy to understand that relationships are affected if we don't know how to deal effectively with it. We have difficulties at work relating to our co-workers, in the classroom being a good teacher who disciplines the students appropriately, at home being lovable and loving, and in religious life learning to express anger in such a way that effective change takes place. In other words, to establish good relationships at work, at play, and at home, it is necessary to tell the person with whom we are annoyed, exactly what was said or done that was upsetting. An extremely important aspect of this sharing is to do it without blaming the other person, without saying, "You're wrong and I'm right." When we communicate our anger, the goal ideally is to share where we are, to inform the other person what's going on inside of us, and not to condemn the other of wrongdoing. For example, if a friend is late in picking me up, one approach is to criticize her all the way to the theater about being the cause for coming late to the movie. A more effective approach is to share my anger because I value seeing the very beginning of a movie and as a result of her coming fifteen minutes late, the movie will be started when we get there. Thus, "I" messages are effective while "you" messages are ineffective because they involve negative judgments.

Anger Expressed In Our Bodies

It's easy to know when we are angry, because when this happens, we want to fight. Our whole system blasts this message home to us, as our bodies are prepared for action. Sugar pours into the system to give us energy. Our blood pressure increases as our hearts beat faster. More adrenalin is secreted, dilating the pupils of the eyes to enable us to fix our eyes more narrowly on the enemy and to help mobilize ourselves in general for action. If there is no release of this built-up energy, we remain in a constant state of readiness to fight, with heart beating rapidly, blood pressure elevated, and chemical changes occurring in the blood. It is clear the body can't withstand this for a long time. Something must give.

When our anger is unexpressed verbally, it often finds a way of expressing itself nonverbally through the body. A tension headache is a common way. Our language even reveals the expression of this anger when we say, "I'm going to blow my stack," and, "I've got to let off some steam." These phrases colorfully describe what's going on within us. Some people describe their tension headache as feeling like there is a very tight skull cap around their head. The pain which seems to go down the back of the neck is sometimes caused by a pinched nerve, but often by muscle tension which results from accumulated anger. This is clearly illustrated when we say, "He gives me a pain in the neck" because then we are accurately describing the situation.

In everyday language we frequently hear the phrase, "I can't stomach that man." How accurate this phrase is, because it means I'm so angry I can't eat anything or accept anything into my stomach to digest. The digestive tract, a thirty foot long tube, is a very common outlet for the emotions when they cannot be expressed in other ways. Some people choose to express their emotions at the end of the tract, the colon. It's easy to recall some vulgar phrases we have in English to communicate our anger which include some mention of the products of the bowel. Some people merely use the vulgar phrases, but others actually develop diarrhea or constipation. This can be traced to our infancy when bowel movements had many meanings. For example, a bowel movement sometimes was a means of pleasing our parents and thereby getting their approval; or when we got angry at them, we soiled our clothes as a safe manner of expressing our anger. Possibly this caused them to be embarrassed, or at least put them to the trouble of cleaning us.

Other common phrases in our language which indicate our bodily expression of anger are: "Don't get your blood pressure up" and "Watch out or you'll blow a gasket." Again, this describes what is happening when we become angry; our bodies are prepared to fight and as a result, our pressure rises. If we don't resolve the anger, then the high blood pressure condition continues and this results in chronic hypertension. A young executive, for example, who is consistently given more work by his boss, becomes very angry because of the excessive workload, but never shares his anger for fear it will hinder his chances of getting a promotion. As a result of his unreleased anger toward his boss, he has high blood pressure constantly and develops chronic hypertension.

The body can also express repressed anger through overeating. This may have developed in early childhood when our parents punished us for the manner in which we ventilated our anger, e.g., kicking the furniture, and unfortunately we got the message that we were unlovable. In order to soothe the hurt, we ate more than usual. As we became adults, we continued to feel bad and unlovable every time we got angry. This naturally resulted in a sense of guilt and depression which we satisfied by overeating, and this over-eating both punished and comforted us. The ultimate result of this pattern was overweight for us.[7]

Other bodily ailments commonly associated with repressed anger are: vomiting, ulcers, respiratory illness, skin diseases, genito-urinary tract diseases, strokes, tics, heart attacks, depression, self-imposed starvation, and either excessive sleeping or insomnia.[8]

In their personal lives, pastoral care people need to learn how to deal with their anger in a healthy manner so that they themselves don't become sick by expressing it through their bodies. In addi-tion, they need to learn the skill of eliciting the repressed anger of others so that they can become productive Christians, instead of people weighted down by avoidable illness. When some persons are hospitalized, they get in touch with their pent-up anger and so welcome assistance in relieving themselves of this poisonous venom.

Hostility, Passive Aggressiveness and Displacement

Our bodies are not the only way repressed anger is expressed. Hostile comments are another unhealthy manner, and the unfor-tunate aspect about it is that we do not admit our remarks have a barb attached to them. When someone confronts us about our hostility, we deny having made the remark or suggest the person is paranoid for such an interpretation. One lady used to hide her hostility toward her husband with a lot of verbiage; she told many stories, but had the uncanny habit of interjecting them with com-ments about widowhood, husbands dying, and insurance policies. She simply could not understand why her husband became irritated when she did this. Another type of hostile person is the one who constantly finds one flaw in everything whether it is a plan, a paint-ing, a house, etc. This kind of person, who might be called the "but person," also does not admit any hostile intent. Some typical state-ments of this nature are: "That homily was good, but too long," "The parish council really works hard, but it's a shame they accomplish so little," "That chaplain is really dedicated to the sick, but she is a workaholic." When others become angry at him for these hostile remarks, he is completely surprised and defends himself saying, "I'm only being honest. You can't get angry at me for being truthful." Actually people are angry at him for his dishonesty, for his disguised anger.

Some other people are more open with their hostility, but still manifest their anger in a distorted fashion. An excellent example of this occurs in the play *Who's Afraid of Virginia Woolf?*. The husband and wife enjoy cutting each other down in the presence of other college professors and their spouses. Everyone knows they are angry with each other, but they never share their anger directly. Instead, they take turns belittling each other, pointing our real and imaginary limitations. Their relationship could deepen if they spoke about their anger and its causes openly.

A devastating hostile expression is to deny the existence of the feelings of another. This hurts deeply because it directly contradicts the other person in the vulnerable area of feelings. This occurs on vacation when a person expresses his fear of climbing to the top of a mountain and his irritated friend responds, "No, you don't. You get a kick out of being up on high ledges." If this happens often, it tends to make a person crazy.

When pastoral care persons accumulate a lot of anger, they may turn the anger in on themselves and become depressed. This depression manifests itself by insomnia, poor appetite, feelings of hopelessness, etc. If this depression becomes acute, a pastoral person can begin to feel worthless, blame himself for everything that goes wrong, and in extreme cases commit suicide, the ultimate hostile action. It is estimated there are about 32,000 suicides annually, but many suicides are never recorded as such. Not only are deaths reported as accidents when they are really intentional, but some persons are unaware they are committing suicide. Sometimes it is pointed out to a reckless driver, "You're trying to kill yourself driving like that and some day you'll succeed." We can only guess at the number of people who die in automobile, boating and swimming accidents and drug overdoses because of their basic wish to kill themselves. Such a drive exists in a number of drug addicts and alcoholics. Alcoholics may be described as "drinking themselves to death," while the same drive may be more subtle in obese persons who are "eating themselves to death."[9]

Another unhealthy method of expressing our repressed anger is through passive actions or comments. Recently, I caught myself doing this playing golf. When a twosome playing behind us became impatient at our slow pace, they played constantly on our heels and then asked to play through us. I was angry with them and didn't want to wait for them to play through us but reluctantly agreed. My passive aggressiveness was displayed when I left my golf cart in the middle of the fairway so that one of their balls might hit it and thus hinder their game. Another familiar manner of being passively aggressive is to refuse to listen to someone with whom we are upset. We can do this gently by simply reading the paper or watching the TV instead of lending the other person our ear.

Many other common ways of expressing passive aggressiveness are: not listening to another by talking excessively about a safe topic, looking bored, falling asleep on another, giving a person "the silent treatment," forgetting a person's name, speaking to another person in a group and avoiding one person whom we do not like, not looking at another when speaking to him, refusing to say hello to another in passing him in the hall or on the street, being unresponsive in sexual relations, and withdrawing from another person emotionally. Possibly the most frequent hostile communication to the clergy happens during the homily on Sunday mornings when some people constantly look at their watches or read the Sunday bulletin.

Some people are unable to share their anger with the person at whom they are angry, and so they blast some other innocent person. A religious sister who is angry at her coordinator might fear expressing it, and so takes it out on another sister who simply disagrees with her. This is called displacement because the anger is on another rather than on the real target. In this situation the person feels some release of the anger, but it is extremely ineffective because the person is often unaware of the real source of her feelings. It is more beneficial to share the anger with the person with whom we are angry; if that is impossible, the next best thing is to discuss the anger with a friend who is willing to understand us.

Pastoral care persons possibly are most tempted to avoid sharing their anger at their bishop, president of a religious community, pastor, or chief chaplain. They are tempted to let their anger out by "forgetting" to accomplish a task on time, making a "digging" remark to the person in the position of authority, or blasting the secretary for a minor mistake instead of sharing their anger with their boss. Naturally these kinds of behavior hinder their ministry.

Some of us by our temperament tend to use these maladaptive forms of sharing our anger more than others. Some tend to become angry very quickly, being natural fighters or hawks. On the other hand, there are others who are doves; that is, by nature they are not inclined to fight and don't like loud voices, shouting, and yelling. A dove is likely to brag he's never had a fight, and when two doves marry, they proudly proclaim on their twenty-fifth wedding anniversary to all their relatives and friends, that they haven't had a fight or been angry with each other in all those years. It's beneficial for us to realize, whether we tend to be hawks or doves, that there is no person who has never been angry. Hawks, in their extreme form, are bullies; they are always pushing people around and so are considered impolite or boorish. Doves, on the other hand, in denying their anger appear as nice guys and nothing seems to upset them. As a result though, such persons take all the garbage that comes down the street. Their only overt response is a smile, but their covert responses are hostility, passive aggressiveness, displacement, and depression.

One hospital chaplain didn't use any of these maladaptive forms when she became very upset with the chief chaplain who made a decision which affected her work, without consulting her first. She tried to visit patients, but gave up because she simply couldn't listen to them, since her whole being was absorbed with her anger at the chief chaplain. Later that afternoon she functioned effectively with the patients, after she demanded a brief meeting with her boss in which she shared her anger and the reason for it.

Thus for anyone to minister effectively in a parish, hospital or nursing home setting, it is essential that the person have the freedom to experience his/her anger, accept it and decide how to express it appropriately.

Samples of Expressing Anger

Having discussed constructive and nonconstructive methods of expressing anger in general, it's time to provide detailed examples of them. The situation is this: Bob and Carl, both priests, have been taking vacations together for years, but this year Bob decides he's going to Europe with a group of his parishioners. Bob, who meets people easily and mingles well in a crowd, doesn't tell Carl for fear it will hurt his feelings. But Carl, who is shy, sensitive and rather introverted, finds out about his plans through one of Bob's parishioners. Naturally, Carl is hurt and doubly so because of the manner in which the information came to him.

Carl calls him about the time for their weekly golf game and Bob begins to excuse himself.

Bob: "Gee, I'd love to go; the weather is going to be nice, but I have a graduation Mass tomorrow night and haven't given a thought to the homily yet. So I better cancel out for this week."

Carl thinks: If you'd spent time on the weekend on that homily you could go. After all, you knew about the graduation Mass for a month.

He says: "I understand, but I'm surprised you put things off until the last minute like this."

Bob thinks: Who asked him to criticize my work habits? After all, this is a big parish, not a small time operation like his.

He says: "I'm really sorry, but this is a large class and I really want to give them a good thought this year, instead of something just off the top of my head."

Carl thinks: That dirty rat, he's going to mess up my vacation this summer and now the golf for this week too.

But says: "Well, if you can't you can't. How long have you known about the graduation?"

Bob thinks: He's nagging me just like my father did.

And says: "Hey, are you offering me unnecessary advice?"

Carl thinks: I guess he doesn't want to be around me any more. He prefers the rich in his parish and the other priests who are big shots.

But he says (sarcastically): "I had no idea how important your graduation was to you this year."

Bob (responding to the sarcasm): "Maybe the sun doesn't rise and set on those kinds of celebrations but they are important to me. After all, I've known most of the graduates for five years now."

Carl thinks: He's getting angry, I'd better cool it.

But he says: "Why don't we forget the whole thing, even forget I called you. O.K.?"

Bob says: "O.K. I'll see you later."

It's obvious that this interaction was far from effective and so now we will have the same interaction, but with a real meeting of the two persons. Carl calls again about the weekly golf game.

Bob again begins to excuse himself: "I'd love to, but I can't because I need to spend time preparing the homily for the graduation Mass tomorrow night."

Carl: "You know, that really upsets me. I was planning on a nice golf game to help me relax."

Bob: "I can understand that because I know you don't like to play alone and now you have nothing to do tomorrow."

Carl: "Besides that, I heard from one of your parishioners, you're not going on vacation with me this year. I heard you're going to Europe with a group from your parish. I feel left out in the cold."

Bob: "O.K. I guess you do."
Carl: "And what makes it worse is that you never told me
           yourself, but I had to find out from someone else.
           This makes me angry because I thought we were
           really good friends."
Bob: "I apologize. I was wrong. I should have told you
           about the vacation, but I didn't. I can see why you're
           mad at me."
Carl: "Well O.K., at least you understand."
Bob: "Yes, it was my fault, but I want you to know that I
           do care about you and consider you a close friend."
Carl: "I'm happy to hear that."
Bob: "I have cleared my calendar for next week and have
           the whole day off. How about if we splurge and play
           18 at the country club and take a cart too."
Carl: "O.K. That'll be good."
Bob: "I'm sorry about the golf tomorrow and the vacation
           for the summer too. Maybe you could go with us to
           Europe or we could take a week's vacation after I
           return."
Carl: "O.K. Let's talk about it more next week. Good-
           bye."

In the first example (the nonconstructive expression of anger)
there was no real meeting of Carl and Bob because the issue seemed
to be Bob's procrastination. However, the real issue was the hurt
and angry feelings Carl was experiencing because he was left out
of Bob's vacation plans and the weekly golf outing. Associated with
this was the issue whether Carl was a close friend of Bob's or not.
In the "good fight" these feelings were clearly communicated and
when Bob acknowledged them, Carl felt much closer to him. Thus,
their relationship deepened. In the first example too, an unwritten
rule or "family secret" is followed: we won't be honest with each
other. The two friends share their anger through hostile remarks
and passive aggressiveness. Obviously their relationship remains
somewhat shallow and could be broken entirely if one or the other

person no longer tolerated the unhealthy methods of sharing anger.

From such an interchange we can conclude three things about a constructive expression of anger. First, it is interpersonal communication. It deepens the relationship because it gives both parties a new awareness of the attitude and feelings of the other. It not only facilitates unclogging future communication gaps, but also increases each person's sensitivity. Second, it facilitates change. It attacks the present method of sharing with each other, and lays the groundwork for new and more acceptable forms of relating. Third, it is informative. Correct details and feelings that formerly were lost or ignored are shared for each person to clearly understand. Often we tend to conceal or distort facts and feelings during an ineffective expression of anger.[10]

Forgiveness and Reducing Our Anger

Anger over a particular issue ought to end at some point. We know this has happened when we have forgiven the other person. However, if we find it hard to forgive and forget, if we carry grudges after we have apparently resolved an issue, it would be profitable to determine what we get out of protracted resentment.

Some people maintain their anger out of a sense of moral righteousness or power, while others do this to avoid a sense of loss or pain. For example, a person who avidly supports abolishing capital punishment may maintain a righteous anger at anyone who disagrees with his high value of a human life. By encouraging anger at his opponents, he feels that he is an outstanding Christian. In divorce proceedings a wife might allow her anger at her husband to reach the point of rage in order to escape facing the reality that she is no longer a married woman.

When one pastoral person says to another, "Drop dead," she doesn't really want the other person to die, but wants him to drop dead for a little while. This is the same as saying "drop dead as long as my anger lasts," which could be ten minutes. When our anger continues, when it keeps feeding itself, when the flame constantly flares up again, there is something wrong.[11]

Sometimes ministers, active in pastoral work, agree that it's best to ventilate anger, but feel "tied up in knots" with the anger they experience toward the former president of a seminary or high school teacher who prompted them to feel they were the scum of the earth. What can these angry people do after all these years? The former authority person is now elderly and would never understand what the anger was all about. So what benefit is there in sharing the anger with that person? The significant aspect of this problem is for them to acknowledge the anger and somehow convey it. They have a choice about sharing feelings. When one minister came to this point, he no longer felt the need to tell the former superior "where to go." The important change that took place within him was that he was in command and could decide for himself, because he was no longer a stranger to his own feelings. In addition, he realized that, even though the former superior's methods were terrible, he was doing what he thought was best with the knowledge of psychology available to him at that time. Thus, some reconciliation was achieved.

A natural effect of experiencing our anger, accepting and expressing it is to bring it to a conclusion. The opposite is also true: an effect of not allowing ourselves to feel our anger is to encourage it to keep simmering and periodically to burst into flames. So sharing anger has the effect of reducing it.

We can also reduce anger or the frequency of the times we become angry by limiting or reducing our expectations of perfection in ourselves and others. Frequently we become angry with ourselves because we don't meet the unreal goals which we establish for ourselves and others. We demand perfection and become upset when that is not attained. So, it is profitable for us to reexamine our expectations of ourselves and others to see whether they are realistic. Sometimes a chaplain becomes angry with a dying patient because he avoids the topic of death and switches the subject to the nurses' failure to answer his light sooner. Valuable questions for the chaplain to ask herself are, "I wonder why he switches the topic to anger at the nurses?" and "Is he discussing his death with someone else?" By reflecting on her expectations she can determine whether they are real or not, and can reduce the frequency of her anger or frustration in working with the patients and the staff too.

A final method of reducing our anger is to share our expectations with others. Sometimes we assume other people know what we want done and what our preferences are, but our assumptions are not valid. We can save ourselves aggravation if we take the time to share our expectations with our fellow workers or the people with whom we are living.

Music was used in the Old Testament by David to quiet Saul's nerves. Our modern rock and roll with its loudness and speed does not quiet us, but rather stirs up our anxiety level and angry feelings. It's good to be aware that constant listening to this type of music keeps us and others in a state of excitement and fosters the violent expression of anger. Movies that are excessively violent tend to have the same effect because they present the actors as models for us to imitate. We not only imitate their style of dress, etc., but also their violent expression of anger. Violent movies can, though, serve the function of assisting us in expressing our anger vicariously, if at the end of the movie it's clearly understood that this expression of anger is a substitute for ventilating our own anger and that we are not to model our lives after the actors in all aspects.[12]

Anger in Children

Children usually do not have the same problem as adults with anger because they are naturally aggressive and express their anger without shame. This is exemplified when they draw violent scenes with their crayons and when they play "good guys" and "bad guys" on the video. Today children are taught to be possibly more expressive of their anger than in the past because they see more violence on TV. It is easily agreed that sixty to seventy percent of the news they see each night is violent. Indirectly the children are then taught that destructive violence is the way to solve problems, e.g., terrorist groups killing officials of various countries as a means of rebelling against the present social system. When children watch a great deal of television, they easily pick up the idea that violence is a way of life, but unfortunately they are never taught how to release their anger except through violence. It does not take a genius to understand that, since kids watch so much violence on television and in motion pictures, they have learned to ventilate their anger through the destruction of property. Copy cat crimes often trace their source to the media which inspired them. We need to teach children that it is O.K. to be angry, but that they must channel it constructively. It is necessary to help children become aware of their angry feelings, so that they experience themselves being angry and then can choose how they wish to share it.

Conclusion

Pastoral care persons function effectively only if they are comfortable with their own anger and with that of other people. If they repress their anger, possibly at God, when they see a young father of three children dying, then their anger might express itself by some bodily ailment or by helping the patient repress his anger toward God. If chaplains are unable to deal with their anger when some doctor intrudes on their visits with patients, they could become depressed and think about terminating their career in chaplaincy because it seems so insignificant when compared to the profession of medicine. One chaplain dealt effectively with his anger in such a situation by talking to the doctor later and ventilating his anger, saying that courtesy demands the doctor at least excuse himself before he interrupts a chaplain's visit. Sometimes patients are very angry because sickness has disrupted their plans. A pastoral person needs to encourage the expression of this anger rather than discouraging it with some pious platitude like, "Everything works out for the best." Pastoral persons minister effectively with children when they seek to interpret the anger expressed in drawings, instead of urging them to draw "nice" things. The same is true for those patients who are furious at the nursing staff for their cold, inefficient care. This kind of patient is assisted best by chaplains who don't defend the staff, but rather listen as the patients ventilate their feelings about their hospitalization. Pastoral people who fear anger might avoid such patients instead of helping them unburden themselves of their pent-up feelings.

Another aspect of our ministry is to teach people to model the "whole Christ" who was meek on some occasions and shared his anger freely on others. It's important for us to encourage that sound theology be taught in religion classes, from the pulpit and in the sacrament of reconciliation concerning anger. It's beneficial for us to model constructive expression of anger by being as comfortable as possible with other people's anger and comfortable enough with our own to experience it, accept it, and decide how to communicate it appropriately.

Footnotes

[1] John Bradshaw, *Healing The Shame That Binds You*, Health Communications, Inc., Deerfield Beach, FL, 1988, pp. 52-53.

[2] Harriet Goldhor Lener, *The Dance of Anger*, Harper & Row, New York, NY, 1985, pp. 1-2.

[3] Fran Ferder, *Words Made Flesh*, Ave Maria Press, Notre Dame, IN, 1986, pp. 76-78.

[4] George R. Bach and Herb Goldberg, *Creative Aggression*, Avon Books, New York, NY, 1974, pp. 39-49.

[5] George R. Bach and Peter Wyden, *The Intimate Enemy*, William Morrow, Inc., New York, NY, 1969, p. 386.

[6] Theodore Isaac Rubin, *The Angry Book*, Macmillan Co., New York, NY, 1970, pp. 165-167.

[7] Jane Templeton, "Get Angry!" *Weight Watchers*, April, 1978, pp. 10-12.

[8] Nancy Shiffrin, *Anger: How to Use It*, Chatsworth: Major Books, 1976, pp. 32-44.

[9] Leo Madow, *Anger: How to Recognize and Cope With It*, Charles Scribner's Sons, New York, NY, 1972, pp. 87-90.

[10] Jane Templeton, *op. cit.*, pp. 10-12.

[11] Nancy Shiffrin, *op. cit.*, pp. 13-14.

[12] George R. Bach, "You Are Aggressive," *Constructive Aggression*, Human Development Institute, Chicago, IL, 1970.

CHAPTER SEVEN

SEXUALITY

S EXUALITY IS PART OF MINISTRY, just as it is part of every aspect of life. God made us sexual beings, and when we are ministering, we relate to others as sexual persons. We can't relate as "things" or only through our ministerial roles, because then we fail to communicate our warmth and compassion. It is important that we pastoral persons are aware of our sexuality and are comfortable with it as we engage in ministry.

The opening paragraph of the document *Declaration on Certain Questions Concerning Sexual Ethics* published in 1976 by the Sacred Congregation for the Doctrine of the Faith, gives us a beautiful approach to sexuality:

> The human person is so profoundly affected by sexuality, that it must be considered as one of the factors which give to each individual's life the principal traits that distinguish it. In fact, it is from sex that the human person receives the characteristics which on the biological, psychological and spiritual levels, make that person a man or a woman, and thereby largely condition his or her progress towards maturity and insertion into society.

The Meaning of Sexuality

These ideas certainly broaden our concept of sexuality. Formerly, whenever the word sexuality was used, it was restricted to genital sexuality. Now with the new concept of sexuality, our understanding is broadened so that it includes four aspects: generation of children, relationship, sensual pleasure, and fidelity.

In the first story of creation, Almighty God made everything including human beings and then concluded his creation by saying, "Be fertile and multiply, fill the earth and subdue it."[1] Here we have the generational aspect of sexuality.

The second chapter of Genesis states that after Adam was created, he was lonely because no one was like himself. He liked the animals, he enjoyed the beautiful scenery with its greenery, but he had no one equal to himself, no one with whom he could really communicate. So the Lord God said, "It is not good for the man to be alone. I will make a suitable partner for him."[2] When Almighty God brought Eve to Adam, Adam said, "This one, at last, is bone of my bones and flesh of my flesh. This one shall be called 'woman,' for out of 'her man,' this one has been taken."[3] This account illustrates the relational aspect of sexuality.

In the Song of Songs we have another aspect of sexuality in the Bible, the erotic and sensual. The Song of Songs gives us an image in some detail of physical love and recognizes the sacredness of that love. Here we see a lover expressing feelings for the beloved which are erotic, human, passionate, and sensuous. Specifically at the beginning of the book the woman says:

> Let him kiss me with the kisses of his mouth. More delightful is your love than wine. Your name spoken is a spreading perfume; that is why the maidens love you. Draw me. We will follow you eagerly.[4]

Later on in the Song the man extols the virtues of his beloved:

> Your lips are like a scarlet strand, your mouth is lovely. Your cheek is like a half pomegranate behind your veil. Your neck is like David's tower girt with battlements; a thousand bucklers hang upon it, all the shields of valiant men. Your breasts are like twin fawns, the young of a

gazelle that browse among the lilies. Until the day breathes cool and the shadows lengthen, I will go to the mountain of myrrh, to the hills of incense.[5]

Then the woman speaks in detail of the charms of her loved one in these words:

My lover is radiant and ruddy; he stands out among thousands. His head is pure gold; his locks are palm fronds, black as the raven. His eyes are like doves beside running waters, his teeth would seem bathed in milk and are set like jewels. His cheeks are like beds of spice with ripening aromatic herbs. His lips are red blossoms; they drip choice myrrh. His arms are rods of gold adorned with chrysolites. His body is a work of ivory covered with sapphires. His legs are columns of marble resting on golden bases. His stature is like the trees on Lebanon, imposing as the cedars.[6]

There is little discussion directly of sexuality in the Gospels, but it is discussed indirectly in Matthew's Gospel when Jesus speaks about divorce. Here there is strong emphasis on fidelity, the fourth aspect, and divorce is frowned upon because it is opposed to this fidelity. When a marriage takes place, the two people are no longer two, but one as a result of God's activity. Once this sacred relationship is created, it cannot be undone. This fidelity is likened to God's fidelity in his love for all humankind. Even though human beings have been periodically unfaithful to God, God has never been unfaithful in his love for them. So the relationship between God and his people is similar to the relationship between a wife and a husband in marriage. The fidelity that God has displayed for his people is the same fidelity expected between a wife and a husband.[7]

Thus, sexuality has four components; it is not coextensive with genitality, but with personality and the whole person. It is not something added to our humanity as if it were something extra, nor is it one component among many others of our human nature. It is a deep mysterious aspect of personality; it is part of our total personhood. Possibly the strongest indication of this is that the first aspect we observe about others is that they are men or women; that is, we observe the sexuality of the other. Associated with that is the fact that the last thing we remember about others is not their name or occupation, but their sex; that is, we remember whether we related to a woman or a man.[8]

Particular Characteristics of Men and Women

If we look at sexuality from another viewpoint, it has four dimensions: the genital, the affective-social, the masculine, and the feminine. In addition to genitality, sexuality includes our attraction for others, our ability to relate to others, to listen with empathy, to accept people as they are, to be compassionate, tender, affectionate, and warm. Closely connected with these qualities are the characteristics which our culture ascribes to masculinity and femininity. In the West, our concepts in this regard have been dominated by a kind of dualism — the body vs. spirit, body vs. mind, and men vs. women. This dualism promotes an anti-sexual, anti-body, and gender divide in which men are portrayed as superior to women. It views women as acceptable when they are faithful wives and devoted mothers or virginal ascetics, in this way overcoming the stereotype of woman as sexual temptress.[9]

As a result of this cultural heritage, we tend to consider men as authoritative, unemotional, logical, and independent, and women as being submissive, emotional, nurturing, and dependent. These so-called masculine and feminine qualities are not really genetically tied to any particular sex. It is healthy for men to be loving, tender, and warm, and for women to be assertive and take initiative. It is good if both men and women are strong and weak, assertive and gentle.

The participants at the Second Vatican Council were sensitive to the changes of sex roles in various societies, and were careful to avoid assigning any characteristics to one particular sex. In their *Pastoral Constitution on the Church in the Modern World* they always address "spouses and parents," without designating special roles to husbands and wives, fathers and mothers. Marriage is described as an intimate union where a woman and a man are "joined to one another in equal affection, harmony of mind, and the work of mutual sanctification." The Church no longer speaks of man as the head of the home and the woman as its heart. As a result of our cultural biases, we tend to attribute certain characteristics to men and others to women. Men in our society are generally encouraged to compartmentalize their experience and to be task oriented, while women are encouraged to centralize and integrate their experiences. For example, if a husband and wife have argued most of the day and the arguments are unsettled at bedtime, the wife is less inclined to have sexual relations than the husband, who sees no necessary connection between the tensions of the day and sexual relations. A woman more often than a man seeks to unify sex and love, and wants to integrate them. She usually seeks signs of love before she engages in genital sexual relations.

Men more easily and frequently dissociate their experiences; they tend to put their experiences in various categories. They also seem more likely to put everything aside while they involve themselves in an experience. They further tend to be more task oriented and more distant from all their experiences — from the totality of their experiences. As a result, men have greater difficulty integrating their experiences than women generally do. For example, men are not as likely as women to look for love in genital relations and more easily separate love and sex. Some men find it very easy to treat women as sex objects, to treat them almost completely in physical terms. Men can dissociate their physical sexuality from the rest of the total person. Women can treat men as sex objects, but not as readily. They tend to view men in their totality. This does not mean in any way that men are better than women or vice versa; it simply means these tendencies exist.[9]

Another difference between the sexes according to some authors lies in how women and men attain intimacy. Erik Erikson believes that after trust is attained in infancy by forming a relationship with a significant other, all development until intimacy (stage six) is toward autonomy and independence. Isolation then is the norm of development for him.

Carol Gilligan and others disagree. They conjecture that such a way of growing may be accurate for men but not for women. They hold that women develop their identity in relationships with others. They believe too that women form their moral ethics in terms of relationship and conflicting responsibilities, while men develop their ethics from universal principles.[10]

Both women and men are adversely influenced by sexism. This causes women often to adopt the role of pleasing, seeking the acceptance of men rather than being the persons they really are. Men who are oppressed by sexism find it difficult to be sensitive, vulnerable, feel, or cry because these qualities would interfere with their self-image as persons in control, who are expected to dominate women.[11]

Early Attitudes Toward Sexuality

As indicated in the opening quotation, attitudes regarding sexuality have evolved over time. The biblical concept of sexuality as we noted earlier, is one of goodness and fellowship, generation, sensuous love and fidelity. The Gospels portray the affective dimension of sexuality when they describe Jesus as a compassionate, gentle, warm, tender, and loving person. Paul in his Epistles speaks positively, but cautiously, about sexuality. He is positive in the sense that he likens the union of husband and wife to that of God and his people. This gives the relationship of woman and man in marriage a certain dignity. He is cautious because he expresses *as a personal opinion* that celibacy is to be preferred to marriage. Here he goes further than Matthew who says that both marriage and celibacy are viable options. Paul makes it clear that Jesus did not prefer one over the other, but in his letter to the Corinthians, Paul adds that sensuous love is dangerous because it has led some to sin. Further, noting the danger of sensuous love he urges Christians to banish mention of sins of sexuality from their talk.

St. Augustine in the fourth century expressed another approach to sexuality which was influenced by his Manichean past. He taught that physical pleasure is sinful and that all sexual intercourse must be procreative. In more detail, he listed a hierarchy with respect to sexual life stating that celibacy or sexual abstinence is excellent, procreative sexual intercourse in marriage is permissible, sexual intercourse in marriage for other reasons besides procreation is slightly sinful, and sexual intercourse outside marriage is mortally sinful. These opinions of Augustine are a definite break from the biblical teachings.[11]

In succeeding centuries the view of Augustine was corrected, but generally the teaching of the Catholic Church on sexuality has been cautious and negative. The Protestant Reformers seemed to have great ambivalence about sexuality. Martin Luther at times was radical and at others times conservative concerning sexuality. John Calvin was more positive than Martin Luther with his emphasis on the companionship of man and woman in marriage. However, he still saw woman's role as subordinate to the man and she was to be his helper and support. Ulrich Zwingli spoke negatively about sexuality and sensual pleasure, and supported the traditional control of man over woman.[12]

Pope Pius XII in 1951 cautioned spouses about excesses in sexuality due to passion when he taught married couples that "as in eating and drinking, so in the sexual act, they must not abandon themselves without restraint to the impulse of the senses." This papal teaching as well as a number of others was rooted in the concept that human beings lost perfect control over their sensual appetites as a result of the original sin of Adam and Eve. It naturally followed that our attitude toward genital sexuality and toward sensual pleasure in general ought to be one which emphasized control. As a consequence, we tended to think of sexuality in terms of an instinct placed in our human nature by God which must be carefully held in check at all times. In other words, we feared our sexuality, lest it would get out of control.[13]

About this same time many Protestant theologians "were moving decisively away from a law-centered act-focused ethics and toward an attempt to base sexual morality more fully on interpersonal considerations. This shift went hand in hand with a new recognition that sexuality is a fundamental dimension of human life..."[14] This means that in the middle of the 20th century, Protestant theologians were emphasizing sexuality positively.

Modern Attitudes Toward Sexuality

Since Vatican II in the 1960's, the attitude toward sexuality and love has likewise changed appreciably in the Catholic Church. In *Humanae Vitae*, Pope Paul VI states:

> This (married) love is first of all fully human, that is to say, of the senses and of the spirit at the same time. It is not, then, a simple transport of instinct and sentiment, but also, and principally, an act of free will, intended to endure and to grow by means of the joys and sorrows of daily life, in such a way that husband and wife become one only heart and one only soul, and together attain their human perfection.

> Then, this love is total, that is to say, it is a very special form of personal friendship in which husband and wife generously share everything, without undue reservations or selfish calculations. Whoever truly loves his marriage partner loves not only for what one receives, but for the partner's self, rejoicing that one can enrich one's partner with the gift of oneself.

This positive attitude toward sexuality was extended by Bishop Mugavero[15] in his Pastoral Letter on "Human Sexuality" in 1976 where he states that sexuality is one of God's greatest gifts to man and woman. He supports this idea by the fact that not only does sexuality prepare a person to enter society by assisting in the maturing process, "but also because it is that aspect of personhood which makes us capable of entering into loving relationships with others." The bishop goes on to note that sexuality demands intelligence, honesty, and sacrifice that might test our maturity, but he quickly adds that this is no reason to fear sexuality. On the other hand, he urges us to embrace it. However, he thinks that we might fear our own inability to regard it as highly as God who made us sexual persons. He concludes his expressions about the ideal attitude toward sexuality by reminding us that both the married life and the dedicated single life are blessed by God. Jesus indicated the dignity of the married life by elevating it to the level of a sacrament, and he himself endorsed the dedicated single life by his own commitment to celibacy, as he went about doing the Father's will.

No one, though, has spoken more clearly or more often in our day and age about the Church's official positive attitude towards sexuality than Pope John Paul II who, at the very outset of his pontificate dedicated his Wednesday audiences for over a year to this subject. He spoke of it in his encyclical on the *Role of the Christian Family in the Modern World* (Nov. 22, 1981):

> Christian revelation recognizes two specific ways of realizing the vocation of the human person in its entirety, *to love*: marriage and virginity or celibacy. Either one is, in its own proper form, an actuation of the most profound truth of man, of his being "created in the image of God."

Consequently, sexuality, by means of which man and woman give themselves to one another through the acts which are proper and exclusive to spouses, is by no means something purely biological, but concerns the innermost being of the human person as such. It is realized *in a truly human way* only if it is *an integral part* of the *love* by which a man and a woman commit themselves totally to one another until death. The total physical self-giving would be a lie if it were not the sign and fruit of a *total personal self-giving*, in which the whole person, including the temporal dimension, is present: if the person were to withhold something or reserve the

possibility of deciding otherwise in the future, by this very fact he
or she would not be giving totally.

This totality which is required by conjugal love also corresponds
to the demands of responsible fertility. This fertility is directed to
the generation of a human being, and so by its nature it surpasses
the purely biological order and involves a whole series of personal
values. For the harmonious growth of these values, a persevering
and unified contribution by both parents is necessary. The only
"place" in which this self-giving in its whole truth is made possible
is marriage, the covenant of conjugal love freely and consciously
chosen, whereby man and woman accept the intimate community
of life and love willed by God himself which only in this light manifests its true meaning.

And in his encyclical *On the Dignity and Vocation of Women*
(Aug. 15, 1988), the Pope clearly defends the equality of man and
woman:

> The biblical text (Gn 2:18-25) provides sufficient bases
> for recognizing the essential equality of man and woman
> from the point of view of their humanity. From the very
> beginning, both are persons, unlike the other living be-
> ings in the world about them. The woman is another "I"
> in a common humanity. From the very beginning they
> appear as a "unity of the two" and this signifies that the
> original solitude is overcome, the solitude in which man
> does not find "a helper fit for him" (Gn 2:20).

Generally, there are two ways of viewing sexuality, especially
genital sexuality. One attitude regards sexuality as a drive which must
be controlled and consequently a great deal of time and energy is
spent on keeping this drive in check. If this is our attitude, we spend
a lot of time being very cautious to avoid situations and persons in
which the drive could get out of control. This attitude fosters repression of our sexuality. We put chains on our sexuality and are
always spending energy being on guard for fear that one of the
chains might break and the drive get out of control.

Another attitude toward genital sexuality is that it is an aspect of human personality which Almighty God has given us. This attitude approaches sexuality as one of the many drives of our human nature. If we have this attitude, we use our energy not to repress sexuality but rather to make good decisions with regard to its use. As a result, we are aware of our many options and are not restricted to one option, constant repression.

A story illustrates these two attitudes toward sexuality. Two monks were walking alongside the road, and they belonged to an Order which viewed all pleasure as sinful or highly suspect. As they were walking, they came to a small lake and wished to cross it. There was a young lady there who also wanted to cross, but had no means to do so. One monk offered to have the young lady cross the lake on his shoulders as he walked across. She accepted his invitation, and after they reached the other side, he put her down and continued on his journey with his monk friend. A mile later, the second monk broke the long silence and asked why the monk carried that young, attractive lady on his shoulder and placed himself in such a serious temptation. The first monk replied, "I put the young lady down a mile ago, but you are still carrying her." The message is that the second monk was fantasizing about the young lady for a long period of time and felt very self-righteous that he did not place himself in such a serious temptation as the first. However, the first monk was man who made a decision among the available options and then forgot about the decision once it was carried out.

Defense Mechanisms

When we become anxious or uncomfortable in a certain situation because of our negative attitude toward sexuality, our defense mechanisms come into play to help us reduce these feelings. These defense mechanisms are often processes by which we defend ourselves against unpleasant feelings that tend to expose an unacceptable aspect of ourselves or threaten our self-concept. These defenses are unconscious mechanisms that we learned over the years to assist us in uncomfortable and threatening situations. To achieve this benefit, these defenses demand a certain price on our part because we waste a lot of time and energy as was illustrated in the previous example. The challenge for us is to become aware when we are using them, so that we are more open to our experiences and have more freedom in making decisions about how we are going to live our lives.

Of all the defense mechanisms, repression is used more frequently in regards to sexuality than the others. We use it to try to exclude certain experiences from our conscious awareness. We still feel sexual, but refuse to admit to that experience, that is, refuse to acknowledge our own sexuality. In other words, when we use repression, we are living in a world of pretense rather than in the real world of which sexuality is a part.[16]

In using repression, we do not choose freely and consciously to use it because that would be a contradiction. Repression is generally an unconscious process. For instance, a man who constantly represses his sexuality, especially the genital aspect, does not consciously choose to run from this aspect of his personality, but his sexual repression is primarily an automatic process. This type of person seldom allows himself to experience any of his genitality, and if his defense mechanism or repression is bluntly pointed out to him he is likely to feel threatened and to respond with greater defensiveness. Such a person has learned and relearned many times that certain experiences are evil, unacceptable, and a good person would never allow them to take place. Such a person might repress these feelings out of fear, for if he admits them, he risks not only rejection from others, but most importantly, rejection by himself.

Another defense mechanism is denial which protects the individual from unpleasant reality by refusing to face it, often by escapist activities like "getting sick" or being preoccupied with work. An example of denial occurred when a woman wore an extremely suggestive dress which was obvious to others. She refused to believe it even when he co-workers pointed it out to her. Religious sometimes deny their sexuality by becoming "workaholics."

Rationalization is a frequently used defense mechanism, a

process by which we mentally manipulate facts in order to avoid seeing the obvious. We rationalize when we wish to abstain from seeing the real issue as it is, and prefer to justify the way we feel or behave with socially acceptable reasons. Here our sexuality is not denied, but we rationalize sexuality so that we don't face it as it really exists. A priest who was counseling a widow over an extended period of time realized that their relationship was moving towards genital activity. Yet, he rationalized their relationship by stating that it was only pastoral care he was offering and, in addition, that this was being done from the motive of love. However, underneath that rationalization, he feared to admit to himself that their relationship had gone far beyond the bounds of counseling and friendship.

Fantasy which promotes escaping reality by running off into the world of dreams is another defense mechanism important to consider. A danger of any genital fantasy is that it can isolate a person from the rest of his/her life. The real danger of fantasy is that it offers a person the illusion of intimate fulfillment, responsibility, and limits which are all real elements of intimate relations with other people. This type of self-deception robs us of one of the real joys of life which God has destined us to participate in, a close relationship with another human being.

A final defense mechanism is sublimation which literally means to lift up or elevate. Sublimation redirects or rechannels one activity which is unacceptable to another which conforms to our value system. If we are using sublimation, we are not only aware of our feelings but decide to use our energy to promote another activity; that is, we rechannel that energy.

In both the celibate life and in married life, sublimation at times is used because all genital urgings cannot be acted upon. In married life, a certain control is demanded of a person's genital feelings. One of the most frequently recommended activities to channel sexual energy is to keep busy in athletics or manual labor. Oftentimes in high school and college, there is a strong emphasis on athletic programs to keep the young people occupied so that they handle appropriately their genital feelings. These genital urgings can also be sublimated so that the energy is used in a research project, in attaining a high level of academic achievement, in engaging in some creative activity, in working with the poor or underprivileged children. Since we are human beings, we choose how and where to expend our energy. If I choose to spend many hours becoming extremely proficient in playing the piano, I cannot spend much time practicing my golf swing. So sublimating our sexual energy in appropriate channels can be very beneficial in assisting our general health and very necessary in promoting our value system. In this way it differs from the other defense mechanisms mentioned.[17]

The Myths About Sexuality

In spite of our efforts to attain a positive attitude and to reduce the use of our defense mechanisms concerning sexuality, we live in a world that has many myths, and especially myths concerning genital sexuality. It is difficult not to absorb some of these myths and begin to assume they are true. Many TV commercials and other advertisements use these myths directly or indirectly, to try to sell their products.

In order to more clearly recognize these myths, it is profitable for us to indicate some of them. The first and possibly most dangerous myth is that man and woman have been destined by God to live forever in complete happiness. This is an impossibility; no human being, including Jesus Christ, has ever been happy all of his/her life. It is impossible to live a life where everything goes right all the time, and maybe it is impossible to live one week where everything goes according to our wishes. Another aspect of this myth is that we can live an anxiety-free life. There are bound to be certain situations that occur in our lives that make us more or less anxious. To support this myth, some of us have the idea that "If I get my Ph.D., or marry this or that person, or take this vacation, or move into this part of town, or buy this automobile, I will be happy." From experience, all of us know that the things we long to attain make us happy and content only for a time, but not forever.

The second myth is that genital sex is a crucial part of being a human person; it's so special that when sex is had, lights will flash, bells will ring, and the person will be in a state of ecstasy. When people have sexual intercourse with these exceedingly high expectations, they generally are severely disappointed. One young man who began having sexual relationships in high school said that he had these expectations and now concludes, "Sex is not such a big deal after all." Eight years later, the same man states that, "Like the rest of life, sex is what you make it. It's not a magical force with its own power to save you, or fulfill you, or whatever. But it took me a long time to sort that out and to stop blaming myself as a failure."

Another myth akin to that one is that genital sex makes people happy. If we are sad, if things aren't going right in our life, then our cultural myth tells us that sex will cure our ills. In reality, there is no one cure for everyone's ills. Sometimes it even happens that people who are sad, become unhappier through genital sex because they feel more lonely than before, because they now feel guilty.

That genital sex means instant intimacy is the fourth myth. Another way of phrasing this is that celibacy is the absence of intimacy. The physical intimacy of sexual relations doesn't guarantee "real intimacy," which is sharing on a deep level with another person. It means sharing feelings, opinions, significant happenings, and goals with one another. A celibate person can share in depth or be intimate with several people, while a married person is not necessarily intimate even with one person.

The fifth myth is extremely common in our American culture, namely that marriage relieves loneliness. If people are lonely before marriage, they are likely to be lonely after marriage. If a person is extremely lonely, it often means that the person has difficulty in interpersonal relationships, and marriage does not solve that, but rather focuses on that problem in a person's life. Physical closeness does not mean loneliness is resolved. How often is it stated that people have been lonely in a crowd, which means that they have not established any close relationships with anyone in that crowd. Besides, loneliness is better tolerated by those who live alone;

they have no expectations about marriage solving their pain of loneliness and so are not disappointed. Lonely people who marry have
about the same chance of realizing their expectations as the host
at a party who insists that everybody have a good time.[18]

The sixth myth is that celibacy is a life of sacrifice. Celibacy
means a life of sacrificing genital sexual pleasure, but there are many
other pleasures available to the celibate person, namely, a certain
independence, and the ability to serve the Lord in a particular way
that one chooses. Another myth is that celibacy and sexuality means
the same thing to everyone. Certainly celibacy and sexuality mean
one thing to one religious woman, whereas to another religious
woman in the same congregation, it may mean something else.
Because of our cultural heritage, celibacy and sexuality often differ
for religious women and religious men. Another aspect is that what
celibacy and sexuality meant ten years ago to a religious person, it
does not mean today. Many religious men and women in their formation days, were given the concepts of sexuality and celibacy that
their founder or foundress had, or the concepts their spiritual director held. As these religious people matured and digested these
concepts, no doubt they changed drastically. These differences in
concepts of sexuality and celibacy are healthy because there are
many different aspects to them.[19]

Affective Sexuality — Intimacy

Rejecting the myth that sexuality is coextensive with genitality,
we are mindful that sexuality enables us to enter other person's lives
as friends and to encourage them to enter our lives. This happens
not by just sharing facts about ourselves, but by allowing people to
know the fears that disturb our quiet moments, the loneliness that
hides behind our smile, and the passions that excite and scare us.
This occurs by revealing secrets about ourselves to those whom we
call friends. Thus friendship occurs by sharing the heart, not exchanging information.[20]

When we have formed intimate relationships, our lives become full and enjoyable and not just an existence. The challenge we have is to transform our lives to make them truly meaningful, to escape the slavery of the ignorance of how to love. In other words, our challenge is to know how to use our sexuality for giving life, for truly loving, for forming deep and lasting relationships. However, to do this, we must trust others and not be fearful of becoming dependent on them. Psychologists state that it is a well known fact that some people have a strong revulsion to sexuality because of their will to be totally independent. So sexuality is that relational aspect of our personality that reminds us of our need for others, of our dependence upon them.[21]

Associated with our fear of dependency on another, is our fear of being swallowed up by them. Many times in marriage or in a close friendship, we will only go so far for fear that if we go further, we will be swallowed up by the other person. Sometimes in marriage, a spouse will mention that she/he is willing to meet half of the other person's needs, but will go no further because the other person constantly will develop new needs, and as a result, the individual will lose his/her identity. This is one of the fears of relating on a close level with another person, or one of the fears of intimacy. One reason we fear losing our own identity is that our identity is unclear and is built on sand. If we are solid in our identity, then this fear decreases.

A beautiful example of the intimacy about which we are talking occurs in the Book of Jonah. There, Jonah is swallowed up by the whale and becomes, as it were, one with the whale, living in its belly. Once he is vomited up by the whale on the shore of Nineveh, he becomes a new person. Before this he was a resistant, fearful person who rejects God's command. Once he experiences intimacy, he is a new individual. Now he is a God-centered, spirit-filled, determined and open person. Intimacy enabled Jonah to become a new person.

In order to understand who we are, that is, to attain a clear identity about ourselves, it is important for us to become intimate like Jonah did. Intimacy is a need that all of us have in order to become whole individuals. This ties in with Jesus' words that unless we lose our lives, we will not be able to have life. In other words, unless we lose ourselves in someone else, as Jonah did in the belly of the whale, we cannot really be our own true person. For by sharing ourselves with another, we come to a greater understanding of who we are as persons. At the same time, there is fear and hope involved. There is fear of being swallowed up by another, the fear of not being able to be free to make decisions for ourselves any more; and there is hope present too, the hope that through intimacy we can grow. Our challenge is to overcome our fear in order to allow ourselves to grow.[22]

Intimacy, is being known and knowing other persons. In this process, we ever so slowly come to believe that certain aspects of our personality or of our bodily image which we find unacceptable, which embarrasses us, can in fact be accepted by others. This acceptance enables us to learn, to own and love our family and personal history with its many wonderful feelings and its pains. This enables us to own our sinfulness. We no longer have a need to be perfect to be loveable. When we have been deeply affirmed by others who really love us, and once we accept that affirmation, then we are on the road to allowing God to love us, precisely because he knows us with our strengths and weaknesses. Thus there is harmony between growth in human and divine intimacy.[23]

When we have attained a deep friendship with another person, we will still experience periodic moments of loneliness because this is part of being a human being. However, our loneliness will not exist for a prolonged period because it results from a lack of contact or linkage with our world. People who are continually lonely are so because they fail to feel in some way that they are having an impact on another, that their being alive makes some difference for some person in the world.

The degree of intimacy or affective sexuality depends primarily on our relationships and motivations. This may involve marital love, a close friendship, a gracious meeting, or a warm recognition. Affective sexual behavior can be an end in itself, or it can be a means of attaining genital gratification. A warm smile or a gentle embrace (affective sexual behavior) can be ends in themselves, or they may simply be the steps that lead to sexual intercourse. Confusion results when all expressions of affection or intimacy are classified as preludes to genital behavior.

The intentions of the people exchanging signs of affection are extremely important in determining whether the affective sexuality is an end in itself or a means leading to genital activity. A difficulty arises when there is a conflict concerning the intentions. A woman may show signs of affection for a man with no intention of this leading to genitality, but her male friend may misinterpret her intention and consequently feel that she is encouraging genital intimacy. On the other hand, a man may have only the intention of showing simple affection to his close friend but then becomes genitally aroused. Here there is a conflict between his intention and his feeling.

Example of Intimate Friendships

Having spoken of the value of intimacy, it is important to see how intimate friendships were viewed in the life of the Catholic Church. Aelred of Rievaulx, a twelfth century Cistercian monk, gives us a beautiful treatise on the subject of friendship. Aelred's discussion is valuable because he is not speaking solely from theory, but his ideas arise out of his own experience in life. His own friendships with Waldef and Walter Daniel are well known. Aelred viewed friendship as a creation of human effort and a gift of God. He discusses friendship in his letter entitled, "Spiritual Friendship" where he writes:

> There is no more powerful, more efficacious, more excellent remedy for our wounds, in everything that comes to pass in this life, than the possession of someone who comes to console us and sympathize with us when we suffer disappointments and comes running to congratulate us when we have met with success. "Two friends," says the Apostle Paul, "help carry one another's burden"

(Gal 6:2). In fact, each finds his own burden smaller than that of the other. Friendship, then, adds light to happiness and alleviates misfortune because it sympathetically shares burdens. Indeed, in this life, a friend is the best remedy of all.[24]

In the seventeenth century, Francis de Sales gives us a much more cautious view of intimate friendships in his book, *Introduction to the Devout Life*. In order to understand the reason for these different approaches, it is important to note that Francis de Sales lived in an entirely different era from that of Aelred of Rievaulx. Francis lived at a time when intimate friendships frequently led to genital activity. So he spoke about the dangers of friendships rather than of their great benefit. This caution regarding intimate friendships influenced the spirituality of the Church through the first half of the twentieth century. Most older religious and priests were trained to be very careful during their formation days about forming particular friendships.

In spite of this, there are many examples of intimate relationships in the Church's history. Possibly the best known is that between Clare and Francis of Assisi. Clare was only eighteen years old when she met Francis and left her home and family to follow him. Although they lived separately, they remained in constant communication with one another. During a visit with Clare at San Damiano, Francis wrote his famous "Canticle of Brother Sun."

There are many other examples of intimate friendship in the Church's history. Famous friendships between men are: Jesus and the disciples whom he loved; Basil and Gregory Nazianzen, Bernard of Clairvaux and William of Thierry, Aelred and Waldef, Jordan of Saxony and Henry of Cologne. There are a number of equally famous friendships between men and women: Catherine of Siena and Raymond of Capua, Francis de Sales and Jane Frances de Chantal, Vincent de Paul and Louise de Marillac, and Teilhard de Chardin and Leontine Zanta.[25]

Such intimate friendships always have their dangers but, at the same time, they are a source of strength, beauty, growth, and ability to love Almighty God. It is simply impossible to love everyone in general when we cannot love anyone in particular.

The Integration of Sexuality

Often when the word "integration" is used, it means that we take something that we know intellectually and move that to what we experience on the gut level. For example, on a theoretical level or the intellectual level, we know that it is better to express our anger to another, but on the gut level it takes some time to feel comfortable in sharing our irritation or anger with another person. When we speak here about the integration of sexuality, we are speaking about this aspect of integration in the sense that we are urging a positive outlook toward sexuality to enable us to feel comfortable with our own and other's sexuality.

Integration in this context also means that we realize that integration means "whole." There is a tendency in our culture to look upon sexuality in a fragmented way — we only look upon the genital aspects of another person rather than consider the whole person who has genital components. For instance, a man might be sexually attracted to a woman and realize that she is well-formed and has beautiful breasts. However, there are no such things as breasts and well-proportioned hips in the abstract, but only as components of a woman who has many other aspects to her personhood. What kind of person is she socially, intellectually, psychologically, and spiritually? If we only look at her physical attractiveness, we are fragmenting her, instead of looking at the whole person; thus we are seeing her purely as a sex symbol, seeing her purely as a physical person rather than understanding her personality strengths, weaknesses, etc.

In order to see persons in their wholeness, it's important for us to look again. We see them originally by what attracts us, which possibly is their physical being. If we take a second look, we see very clearly other aspects of the whole person. Sometimes women nurses make comments about a male patient, speaking about how broad a chest the young man has, how nicely formed the hair is on his chest and that it's not too much hair so as to look like a bear, but just a sufficient amount to make him sexually attractive to them. When they talk about him only in this light, they are looking at him from a very narrow viewpoint, instead of seeing him as a total person with a spiritual, intellectual, social, and psychological dimension.

Speaking of integration, we don't want to confine it to the total person either. We choose also to look at the total relationship. Sometimes we might not only isolate a physical aspect of an individual, e.g., a woman's breasts or a man's hairy chest, but also one individual act and not evaluate that act as part of a total relationship. In fantasy, we might imagine having genital intercourse with a person who is not our spouse and daydream how pleasurable that would be. Integrating our sexuality, we realize that this act is not going to end with a walk into the sunset with our partner, living happily ever after. This genital act cannot simply be totally forgotten. And what about the future of this relationship with the other person? Is there any possibility of marriage, and if there is, can this marriage be a happy union in which there is much more involved than just genital activity? Are we in any way compatible psychologically, intellectually, emotionally, spiritually? We have a tendency to isolate acts and buy into the movie theme that we're simply going to live happily ever after without realizing all the ramifications of an individual act. As mature individuals, we look upon sexuality as being part of a total relationship with another individual rather than as the whole relationship with another person.

Integration means that we not only have a positive attitude toward all aspects of sexuality, but that we view other people as whole persons instead of viewing simply fragmented sexual parts of them. It means that we realize that genital activity has many implications attached to it, including its psychological and spiritual aspects. Often in experiencing genital urgings, we experience a desire not so much for genital intimacy as for psychological and spiritual intimacy with another person. So, it is profitable to investigate our genital feelings and to understand what they are really trying to tell us.

Psychosexual Maturity and Immaturity

When we have integrated our sexuality into our total personhood, we look beyond the physical attractiveness of an individual and see the total person. This does not mean that we deny the physical attractiveness of others, but we see more than that. It means that in expressing our sexuality, we are not limited to the genital, but relate to others in many different ways.

If we are psychosexually mature persons, we easily admit loving other individuals and do not attempt to make that love abstract by saying that we love humanity. Nor do we attempt to spiritualize that human love by saying simply that we are just following the command of Christ to love everyone. Because of our maturity, we admit that we are attracted to others and have a deep relationship with them to the point that we say that we love them. In this deep relationship, we are able to be intimate without dominating them, without attempting to possess them, to control or manipulate them, without being jealous of their time and their association with others. We are aware when problems arise within our relationships and seek appropriate assistance.

It seems that the more mature we are, the more unity there will be between our espoused values and our private thoughts and behavior. We prize our values highly and treat them with respect. These values are not based solely on authority, and so we don't respond simply out of obedience. These values can stand on their own apart from any authority, but we are open to the guidance of persons in authority. Finally we realize our values are in process, that is, alive and active, not static. Thus, we commit ourselves to certain values, know how to cope with conflicts in our lives, and assume responsibility for the consequences of our choices. If we violate a certain value, we do not immediately blame someone else or the instincts of nature.[26]

In visiting the sick, we are aware when we feel attracted to a certain person, or when a patient or a relative of a patient is attracted to us. One woman chaplain was visiting a dying cancer patient and the husband was usually present. During the first few visits the husband told her of his difficulties managing at home without his wife, his loneliness, etc. He invited her to come to his home at night so that she might cook supper for him and perform some household chores. Immediately, she perceived all this was a cover-up for his interest in her sexually and not as a pastoral minister. Because of her awareness of his covert expressions she told him, "No," and further made it very clear that she was a ministerial person whose ministry was limited to the hospital setting. At the same time, she did not run away from this man, but continued to visit him and his wife. A male chaplain was asked by a female patient, "Tuck me in and kiss me goodnight." An immature chaplain would have run away from the situation in his anxiety, but this chaplain sat down with her and initiated a conversation about how lonely she was as a single person and later in the visit how much she wanted to be married.

Fr. Donald Goergen indicates these as signs of psychosexual maturity: 1) the capacity to love myself; 2) the capacity to love persons of the other sex; 3) the capacity to love persons of my own sex; 4) the capacity to love God; 5) the capacity to love in a non-possessive way; 6) the capacity to love physically; 7) the capacity to communicate tender and warm feelings; 8) the capacity for genital love and orgasm; 9) the capacity to distinguish sexual desire and sexual love; 10) the capacity to integrate sexual desire into a loving relationship.[27]

Psychosexually immature pastoral persons compensate extensively in thought, affect, and behavior. One form of compensation occurs when they participate vicariously in the heterosexual activities of their parishioners or patients. They may encourage patients to speak often or in great detail about their genital activities, and compensate in this way for their lack of genital expression. Another form of compensation happens when they take a great deal of interest in the struggles that celibates have in remaining celibate. When the conversation constantly revolves around sexual matters, it usually is a sign of immaturity.

Another form of compensation is to deny or demean the value and pleasure of genital expression. Celibates are tempted to deny the legitimate value of genital expression or to make fun of it, and in this way, indicate their lack of psychosexual maturity. Others compensate by taking refuge in genital fantasies which offer them gratification through vicarious conquests. This is simply substitution. Celibates who frequently use compensatory measures are struggling intensely with the challenges of celibacy, and their ministry is hampered as a result.

When priests, sisters, and seminarians regard celibacy as an excessive burden and feel that the Church is depriving them of a legitimate avenue of communication by *imposing* celibacy on them, their pastoral effectiveness is limited. This feeling of being "cheated" because of the Church's law expresses itself as these people minister in their various settings, e.g., "poor me." These people are psychosexually immature, and need to work through these feelings of anger at the authorities of the Church and of being "unjustly" deprived of genital expression. Such persons experience severe internal conflicts, and their immaturity influences their behavior to the extent that they frequently seek gratification covertly.[28]

Sometimes immature pastoral care persons express their immaturity by denying their sexuality and the sexuality of the persons to whom they are ministering, and other times by simply being naive. One woman student chaplain visited a 65-year-old widower who frequently bragged about his three different girl friends visiting him during his hospitalization. He urged her to visit him daily saying, "Come every day. You make me feel better." This student presented her conversation with him as a verbatim to her peers for feedback. When one of them asked if she felt he was flirting with her, she was surprised that any student would bring this up. She denied that he would have any motive like that, and felt that he just enjoyed her ministry but did not relate to her as a sexual person.

Another example of immaturity occurred in my own life as a student supervisor. I appeared before a committee requesting a feedback on how I had supervised five students. One of the committee persons asked me how I felt about a particular woman student I had. I answered him in a very vague way and said that I had no particular feelings about her, even though he knew that she was an attractive woman. He began pushing me, "Did she turn you on? Was she sexy? What kind of legs did she have?" These questions embarrassed me and I was unable to respond. This was because I was too immature to admit that I was a sexual being and found this woman student attractive.

Another example of how a person's immaturity affected ministry occurred with a student chaplain. Initially, he came to the program dressed in a shirt and tie, but then during the third week of the program discarded that attire and began coming to the program with an open shirt with his hairy chest showing. When people commented about this sporty, sexy attire, he denied this and claimed that it was just too hot to wear a shirt and tie. It was difficult to accept this denial, because the room where we had our classes and the hospital where he visited patients were air conditioned. This student was expressing his psychosexual immaturity by seeking the women's affirmation of him as a sexual person.

One or two actions do not indicate that we are psychosexually immature. But there are some general indicators of our maturity or immaturity. From her experience as a woman religious and a psychologist, Sr. Susanne Breckel thinks that these are signs of a person's psychosexual immaturity: 1) awkward around people of the opposite sex, e.g., don't know where to put feet or what to say; 2) must be around "the boys or girls" all the time and is uncomfortable being alone; 3) hides behind his or her role and is never seen as a real person; 4) relates as a "thing" to others rather than as a man or a woman; 5) relates to people as a super intellectual and only relates to others from the head up. She goes on to say that sometimes this immaturity is displayed through chemical dependency on drugs or alcohol and other times it's expressed through an excessive interest in sports or a person's work. She concludes that any excessive interest in a particular area is a possible sign of a person's immaturity.[29]

Principles Concerning Sexual Transgressions

It is important for pastoral persons to reflect on transference and counter-transference because they are operative in ministry. Transference occurs when parishioners "transfer" their feelings, expectations and behaviors from previous relationships to the pastoral persons currently involved in trying to be of help. For example, a woman who has learned to be very submissive to demanding parents tends to be submissive to pastoral persons. A man who has learned consistently in childhood not to trust his mother probably will have difficulty later trusting a pastoral woman. An adult who has learned from childhood that one's parent is always available to offer support in times of trouble, will expect a similar support from pastoral people. The more emotionally laden the pastoral situation is, the more likely it is that transference will occur. When a wife is at the bedside of her dying husband and is comforted by a male pastoral person, it is possible for this grieving woman to experience, under these circumstances, more intense feelings toward the caring minister than normal.

Counter-transference, on the other hand, happens when the recipient of ministry places feelings, expectations, or behaviors on pastoral persons and they, in turn, transfer their emotional needs and feelings to others, for example, their parishioners. Counter-transference is often unconscious, and obviously impairs effective ministry. Ministers lose their objectivity in the situation. When a man in crisis transfers to a woman chaplain his yearning for motherly care, the chaplain might be over-protective in her ministry because of her own need to be motherly. When a young woman transfers to a lonely priest her need for acceptance and love, the priest might misinterpret her feelings as true love for him.

There are two principles operative in discussing boundary violations of a sexual nature. First, the professional always has more responsibility than anyone else. The burden is on pastoral persons to maintain a professional relationship with the patient or family. The same is true for a doctor in a doctor-patient relationship. The doctor has the greater obligation to maintain a professional relationship rather than to allow it to become a personal one in which the patient is harmed. Transference and counter-transference might explain how a professional relationship deteriorated into a sexual one in which the individual was harmed, but this does not absolve the professional from responsibility.

Second, sexual activity between a professional and a patient is always harmful to the unsuspecting individual. This principle is based on the power differential between the professional and the recipient of care. In such a situation consent to sexual activity is usually never free or mutual, because the recipient is influenced by transference. Sometimes both persons will feel that their emotional attraction is equally consented to; at times the client may desire or even initiate the seduction. The relationship is still not equal and the recipient of pastoral care is not free.

When transference is operating, the relationship between pastoral persons and stressed persons is often similar to that between a parent and a child. On this level, needy persons are anxious to please the comforting mother or father figure in any manner which that person requests. Later clients may experience feelings of shame or ingratitude about feelings of revulsion or resistance to what was asked of them. These same individuals might also feel guilty about cooperating in the sexual activity and blame themselves totally for what took place.[30]

In conclusion pastoral care persons need to be aware of their sexuality in order to minister effectively. They are constantly relating to people, not through their role, but as human beings who have a sexual dimension. It is important for them to have close friends and a strong support system so that they can live life to the fullest and have their needs for intimacy met in these relationships rather than through taking advantage of those who come to them for care and help.

Footnotes

[1] Genesis 1:28.

[2] Genesis 2:28.

[3] Genesis 2:23.

[4] Song of Songs 1:2B-4D.

[5] Song of Songs 4:3-6.

[6] Song of Songs 5:10B-15.

[7] Donald Goergen, *The Sexual Celibate*, Seabury Press, 1974, pp. 14-25.

[8] Beverly Wilding Harrison, "Human Sexuality and Mutuality," *Christian Feminism*, Judith L. Weidman, Ed., Harper & Row Publishers, San Francisco, CA, 1984, pp. 147-148.

[9] Beverly Wilding Harrison, *op. cit.*, pp. 142-143.

[10] L. Patrick Carroll and Katherine Marie Dyckman, *Chaos or Creation*, Paulist Press, New York, NY, 1986, pp. 50-51.

[11] Rosemary Radford Ruether, *Sexism and God Talk*, 10th Edition, Beacon Press, Boston, MA, 1983, pp. 185-190.

[12] Nancy Tuana, *The Less Noble Sex*, Indiana University Press, Bloomington, IN, 1993, pp. 12-14.

[13] William C. McFadden, "Sexuality and the Church," *America*, October 21, 1978, pp. 262-265.

[14] James B. Nelson, *Between Two Gardens*, 5th Printing, The Pilgrim Press, New York, NY, 1990, pp. 65-95.

[15] Bishop Francis J. Mugavero, "Pastoral: Human Sexuality," *National Catholic Reporter*, March 5, 1979, p. 8.

[16] John Bradshaw, *Healing The Shame That Binds You*, Health Communications, Inc., Deerfield Beach, FL, 1988, p. 74.

[17] William F. Kraft, *Sexual Dimensions of the Celibate Life*, Kansas City, MO: Andrews and McMeel, Inc., 1979, pp. 66-82.

[18] William J. Lederer and Dr. Don D. Jackson, *The Mirages of Marriage*, W.W. Norton & Co., New York, NY, 1968, pp. 75-78.

[19] John J. Malecki and Susanne Breckel, "Sexuality: The Celibate Response," *National Assembly of Religious Brothers*, Passionist Broadcasting, West Springfield, MA, 1978, Tape 1.

[20] Fran Ferder, *Words Made Flesh*, Ave Maria Press, Notre Dame, IN, 1986, pp. 171-173.

[21] Theodore W. Jennings, "Theological Perspectives on Sexuality," *The Journal of Pastoral Care*, March 1979, p. 5.

[22] Mary Elizabeth Kenel, Ph.D., "A Celibate's Sexuality and Intimacy," *Human Development*, Spring 1986, pp. 14-19.

[23] Bernard J. Bush, "I Have Called You By Name," *Intimacy*, Anna Polcino, Editor. Affirmation Books, Whitinsville, MA, 1978, p. 48.

[24] Aelred of Rievaulx, "Spiritual Friendship," 2nd French Translation in *The Library of Medieval Spirituality*, Brussels, 1948, pp. 53-57, and "The

Friendless Man is Truly Alone," *Christian Readings*, Vol. 4, Year 1, Catholic Book Publishing Co., New York, NY, p. 71.

[25] Rubert Murry, "Spiritual Friendship," *The Way*, Supplement 10, 1970, pp. 61-73.

[26] William F. Kraft, *op. cit.*, pp. 85-93.

[27] Donald Goergen, *op. cit.*, pp. 178-179.

[28] Philip D. Cristantiello, "Psychosexual Maturity in Celibate Development," *Review for Religious*, September 1978, pp. 652-654.

[29] John J. Malecki and Susanne Breckel, *op. cit.*, Tape 1.

[30] Jane F. Becker, O.S.B. and David S. Donovan, S.J., "Sexual Dynamics in Ministry Relationships," *Human Development*, Fall, 1995, pp. 23-27.

CHAPTER EIGHT

GROUPS

TODAY WE FORM GROUPS AND have meetings about almost ev-thing. Pastoral persons need to be aware of the dynam-ics that are taking place in meetings and how to intervene effectively to assist the members in attaining their goal. Knowledge of group dynamics was important to me in a recent meeting which I had with the personnel of the labor and delivery department to discuss our practice of baptizing newborn infants at the hospital.

The meeting for the night and day shifts began at 6:30 a.m. with the head nurse introducing me to the group. I explained to the nurses that the Catholic Church has undergone some changes since the Second Vatican Council and one of the changes concerned the sacrament of baptism. Formerly, the Church urged us to bap-tize every dying infant, no matter what the parent's religion, be-cause the baby has a right to heaven which could only be attained through baptism. Now, as a result of new insights, the Catholic Church suggests that we baptize only those babies whose parents wish it and that we offer a prayer over a stillborn infant, rather than baptize a dead person.

After an explanation of the change in policy regarding bap-tism, I asked for comments or questions. Initially there was a pe-riod of silence which was broken by the head nurse, who asked if there were some nurses who might want to comment on this change. A staff nurse spoke up with this encouragement and firmly denounced such radical ideas, claiming that they were completely contradictory to what she was taught as a student in nursing school. The more she spoke, the angrier she became. When she stopped, another nurse chimed in that the Catholic Church has changed enough, and she didn't want any more changes. Another staff member followed by stating that there was nothing wrong with their present policy, and she didn't intend to change in spite of what I said.

At this point I asked the value of giving sacraments to a dead person and how they would feel if a minister performed a religious ceremony for their child without their knowledge or against their wishes. Several other nurses responded that prayers are valuable at any time by anyone, and went on to comment how much damage this new teaching would have on Catholic patients, who would not agree with this radical practice. No one even hinted that this new policy might have any good aspects to it, while several seemed relieved to know it was not sinful if they continued their practice of baptizing all critically ill babies.

This is an example of one group interaction, and what happened in that group happens in many groups. It's beneficial for those who lead groups to understand their dynamics; it's beneficial for persons who participate in many groups (parish council, worship committee, finance committee, education committee, etc.), to know about group dynamics such as the one just mentioned.

Benefits of a Group Decision

One of the shortcomings of the past in the Church's life has been the fact that bishops and pastors made decisions all by themselves. In so doing they never benefited from the skills that lay persons could bring to the situation. Today this has been remedied by establishing pastoral councils, building committees, and many others. Ideally in these groups input is obtained from various people with different backgrounds, and so the group benefits from many experiences and skills of a variety of people. It is true that "many heads are better than one," but it is not beneficial just to empha-

size pure numbers on a committee without any emphasis on quali-
fied people to assist in searching for the best decisions.

When we function autonomously, we become narrow-minded
and easily get into a rut. In the group process, new blood is brought
to the situation and assists in attaining a fresh look at the problem.
In the Professional Advisory Committee which assisted me in performing self-study of the Clinical Pastoral Education program at the
hospital, persons from the following departments were members:
administration, social service, nursing service, staff education, and
field education from a local seminary. These persons brought different backgrounds to the committee and were excellent in preparing for the site visit by an accreditation team of Clinical Pastoral
Education. Their variety of backgrounds offered far more help than
if the committee were composed entirely of clergy persons.

Another benefit in shared decision-making is that it assists
people in accepting the decisions. Persons want to become meaningfully involved in solving their own problems and in making decisions that affect them. When persons do not participate, they tend
to react; they attack, complain, and look for a scapegoat. On the
other hand, when persons help share the events and decisions which
influence their lives, they more readily accept those decisions. When
a bishop made a decision and then made it known to the priests
and laity of the diocese through regular chancery letters and the
diocesan weekly newspaper, the response was often indifference
or angry criticism. At this point too, the bishop had to share his
plan with the priests and laity. He had to spend time explaining his
reasons for choosing his particular plan, and the means he chose
to attain his goal. Later, if the bishop's plan was not successful, it
was easy for everyone to blame the bishop for the failure instead
of taking some responsibility themselves. Presently, if the parish
council is not working effectively, the priest and laity are less apt to
blame the persons they elected to that council, and more likely to
put forth a great deal of effort to make the project succeed.

Finally, group participation assists persons in understanding
the decision and the means necessary to implement it. They know
the other alternatives that were rejected because they seemed to

have less advantages. So they are more convinced that this choice is the best one and are more motivated to see that the goal is achieved.

When the liturgy changes came after the Second Vatican Council, the priests were not involved in making any of these changes and often did not understand the reasons behind them. They simply were told to carry them out. Frequently priests unfortunately modeled that approach with their parishioners and just announced that Mass would be in English, the altar would be turned around, guitars would replace quiet services, and congregational singing would replace silence, and sometimes even the church choir. Neither the priests nor the people were adequately prepared for these changes and as a result, both often felt forced to implement something they did not understand or accept. Naturally, this did not enable them to receive the changes with an open mind.[1]

Essentials For Group Effectiveness

Listening and communicating are essential elements for the effectiveness of any group. Each person has the obligation to listen to what the others are saying and to ask questions to clarify the message. Naturally, if we are simply waiting until the other person stops talking so that a rebuttal can be given, there is little listening. We cannot truly listen if we are formulating our response to the other person's statement. The characteristic required is openness to the ideas and feelings of the persons in the group. A closed person is not really capable of listening. In the initial interaction with the nurses in labor and delivery about baptism, I question how much listening took place and how open some nurses were to new ideas because of the many years this policy has been in practice, and because of their identification with mothers whose infants were critically ill or had died.

Associated with listening is the ability to communicate clearly. Sometimes we fail to communicate clearly because we have not thought through our ideas thoroughly ourselves. As a result we express them in a confusing manner. Other times we fail because we are not in touch with our own feelings, so naturally cannot share them. Another reason for our lack of communicating effectively is fear that our ideas and feelings will not be accepted. As a result, in expressing them we are very anxious and possibly skip some aspect of our message which prevents true communication. Trust needs to be established before much sharing can occur. The group members need to trust each other enough to share ideas that might be controversial. The members need to feel sufficiently safe in their group that they can reject another person's idea, but not the person. The assigned leader can foster this trust by initially explaining how to *confront* others without *attacking* them. The leader can also foster trust by positively reinforcing behavior that leads to a healthy atmosphere in the group, and by not reinforcing behavior that leads to an unhealthy atmosphere. Giving the students adequate information and establishing some structure further enhances the students' feelings that the group is a "safe place" and reduces their anxiety. Generally, more growth occurs when persons feel that there is a safe and protective atmosphere than when they feel threatened and highly anxious.[2]

An essential element in facilitating trust is addressing the issue of confidentiality. The group members need to know that what takes place in the group will not be discussed in the cafeteria at the lunch table, nor with people outside the group. There has to be an agreement that what happens in the group stays in the group.

Another essential element is cooperation, instead of competition. When a group is cooperating, their behavior is directed toward common goals rather than toward each individual's personal agenda at the expense of the rest. Often in the initial stages of negotiation between union and management, much competition rather than cooperation is experienced. Each side appears competitive, striving to achieve its goals at the expense of the other.

When competition prevails in a group, threats and bluffs are used instead of genuine concern for seeking the best possible solution to a problem. Illogical as well as irrational arguments are used rather than logical and innovative considerations. Misrepresentation of one's own needs and not allowing others to know exactly what is wanted and how much one is willing to give up to obtain it are present, instead of an open and honest representation of one's needs. During this period of competition, individuals or factions of the group make themselves appear better than others. There is an emphasis on superiority versus inferiority, an emphasis on "us" vs. "them." There is also a tendency to distort perceptions of others; people perceive they understand the other person's thoughts and feelings, but in reality they don't. In this atmosphere there is a distortion of judgments; one tends to evaluate one's contributions as the best and to downgrade the others. In general, competitive members are so eager to attain their goals that they stereotype other persons, ignore their ideas and feelings, and increase the level of hostility. On the other hand, in an atmosphere of cooperation attention is given to others, communication and understanding prevail, and group support is present rather than individual defensive reactions. The members who have the spirit of cooperation avoid judging others, interact empathetically with each other, and openly share their feelings.

Competition is important in many aspects of our lives, e.g., in business, sports, etc. However, in a group where the members need to work together to attain a common goal, cooperation is essential because the members need to utilize all their abilities to reach the goals of the group.

Leader of Groups

All of us at one time or another have encountered authoritarian leaders. These individuals leave no doubt who is boss. They might be termed the "ramrod" decision-makers. They trust only their insights and think that a group is a waste of time. Their idea of a successful meeting is one in which they manipulate the group to agree with their ideas by the open or subtle use of power. These persons are insecure and so keep as much pertinent information and influence to themselves as possible. They understand only one type of meeting, a win-lose situation, and of course, they always want to win. They abhor indecisiveness because it appears to them as weakness. They detest committees because they seem slow and inefficient.

A second type of leaders are the "contented-cow" decision-makers. These are the persons whose highest value is agreement. Peace at any price is the motto of these individuals who fear conflict, thinking that it results only in hurt feelings and alienation. They presume that no good will ever come from conflict. These persons function on the analogous premise that the contented cow produces more milk. They operate on the principle that it's more important to keep harmony in the group than to come up with the best possible solution. Thus in the group the task is cooperation and avoidance of conflict. Such persons are "nice guys" who are always pleasant and smiling, but nobody knows what they really think because they avoid sharing personal opinions. It's hard to get angry at such persons because they are so nice, yet it's easy to become enraged at them because the members of the committee are dealing with a thing, a non-person rather than an individual who has feelings and ideas.

The third style of leaders are the "cop-outs." These persons don't believe in groups, nor in shared decision-making. They prefer to make decisions alone, but since that is impossible, they tolerate groups. They also abhor disagreement and shun conflict at all costs. As a result, they sit on the sidelines, hoping the meeting will soon be over and that somehow everyone will leave the meeting happy and on friendly terms. These individuals don't make any contributions normally, but if a conflict arises they might suggest that an outside arbitrator be brought in to restore peace to the group.

The "tongue-in-cheek" decision-makers manifest yet a fourth style. These persons want their way, but realize that shared decision making is the "in thing" and so they go along with it. They seem willing to confer, to share with others, to modify their positions to reflect the other persons' viewpoints, but these things are done to gain agreement with "tongue-in-cheek," not because they believe the modifications are an improvement on their original proposal. Their goal before a meeting is to figure out how much they must give up to have the majority approve of their ideas. They are closed to new insights, and are interested in only getting their ideas accepted by the majority. Since there is a great emphasis on "the majority rules," these persons appear very democratic and seem to follow the American way of life.

The final style of leadership in groups is to be found among those who are the "creative" leaders. These persons sincerely believe in the value of groups and want to have the assistance of others in making a decision. They are secure in themselves and realize they don't have all the answers, so they are anxious to have input from others. These persons are aware of their own giftedness and of their limitations, so they seek to improve decisions by having the assistance of others who have knowledge and abilities which they don't possess. They also know that sometimes in the group process, conflicts occur, but they view conflict as the breeding ground for new ideas. These persons believe in the creative potential of the members of any group, rather than fearing others or seeking to pacify those who might disagree with one another.[3] Thus, effective leaders are persons who are caring, emotional, and stimulating, and who offer meaningful contributions and perform executive functions well. Caring leaders offer support, praise their members, accept others and different viewpoints, possess warmth, and protect those persons who might be injured excessively in the group process. When a supervisor performs these tasks, she/he helps instil trust in the members. Emotionally stimulating leaders are those who are challenging, appropriately confrontational, and who share their own opinions and feelings. Those leaders offer meaningful contributions who explain, clarify, interpret, and translate feelings and experiences into meaningful ideas. The leaders who perform the executive functions well are those who set limits, have rules and goals, manage time well, intercede effectively, and analyze the dynamics appropriately.[4]

Individual Group Members

In every group different personalities influence people to act differently. Some of the different kinds of people present in groups are: the aggressor, the distractor, the peacemaker, the clarifier, the blocker, the evaluator, the giver of information, the giver of advice, the information seeker, the giver of support, and the silent observer. It's profitable to reflect on the initial example of group interaction at the beginning of this chapter to see the various roles of these different members. In the sample group, the head nurse functioned as the structurer by introducing me as the speaker for the meeting, calling the meeting to order, coming with an agenda for the meeting, and appointing a person to take the minutes. She also functioned as the initiator by inviting her personnel to voice their opinions when there was silence. The secretary for the meeting adopted the role of a clarifier so that she could accurately take minutes. The first nurses who spoke in the meeting adopted the role of aggressor with their emotional responses. I saw myself function as reflector by asking the nurses the value of continuing their practice of baptizing babies who were already dead, and as an evaluator by asking how they would feel if some minister of a different religion performed a religious ceremony over their child without their consent. At the end of the meeting, when I shook hands with the nurses who strongly opposed any change of policy I was saying, "I reject your idea, but I accept you." I felt like a peacemaker.

Interestingly in this group interaction no one attempted to be the supporter, pointing out one good feature to the suggested policy, and a number sat in silence playing the role of observer. Another noteworthy fact of that experience is that the head nurse did not assume the role of the expeditor to move on to another item on her agenda, but allowed the conflict to continue because it was important for the nurses to express themselves.

We can all remember meetings where someone dominated. I have been to meetings where the pastor dominated the proceedings and if someone voiced an opinion he did not like, he became a blocker. I know of one who blocked a suggestion he opposed by telling the people simply that he would retire from the parish if they insisted on having their way. No doubt you have been at other meetings where there were recognition seekers who always wanted it known how much and how many years they have worked for the parish. Finally, every committee seems to have a distractor who goes off on a tangent giving a lengthy, dull explanation of something the people already know, or of something not pertinent to the discussion. As a result, the members are anxious to continue with the next item on the agenda.

Silent observers do not interfere verbally with the functioning of the group, but they seem to receive a lot of attention from the other members who sit there and wonder about the silence. What does it mean? It could mean many things. Maybe they are angry about something happening in the group or at someone in the group. On the other hand, maybe they are fearful. When a turtle feels threatened, he pulls his head inside his shell. Human beings act the same way. When they are afraid, they withdraw within themselves and shut themselves off from the fearful outside world. Silence could mean they are concerned about appearing foolish because they are unsure of the appropriate thing to say. Maybe it means that there is not sufficient trust in the group for the members to express conflicting ideas. Or it may mean they are uncertain about what is expected of them, and so confusion causes some members to be silent.

The leader or a member of the group may invite the silent members to explore what their silence means, but leaves them free to remain silent. Do the persons need an invitation to share with the group? Some members may say how the silence affects them. Others may say that they feel cheated that they know almost nothing about the observer, or they may resent the fact they risk to share themselves while these individuals just observe. Finally silent members need to know that others will not know of their involvement unless they express it in words.[5]

Another kind of group member is the extremely dependent person who is willing to "rubber stamp" anything someone suggests.

This kind isn't helpful to any committee because she/he looks to others to solve all the problems and to initiate new ideas, while never challenging any suggestions. Such people may look to the clergy person to determine how they should think on a particular issue and then echo those sentiments.

Finally in every group an unassigned member takes on a leadership role. Some of the factors that cause an individual to emerge as the leader are: their leadership qualities, alliances that occur within the group, knowledge and experience of groups, and assertiveness. Generally in every group someone emerges as the unassigned leader and other members fall in line depending on how assertive or passive they are. This person is very influential in the group, depending on her/his attitude toward the group and the whole C.P.E. process. That individual can set a positive atmosphere, or a negative atmosphere in the group which may stifle its life. One of my former students was a dark cloud hanging over the group for most of its existence. He didn't want to take the C.P.E., but was forced to before ordination. He didn't think he could learn anything from the group and was "too tired to put much energy into the C.P.E. process."

As a result of the various kinds of people who make up a committee or group, conflicts naturally arise. It's important how these conflicts are handled. One should not act as if differences don't exist and pass on to the next point on the agenda. Because of the tension resulting from the unresolved conflict, the members won't be able to devote their full attention to the next issue. Another ineffective manner of dealing with a conflict is to allow the parties to engage in a "win/lose" battle. In this case the persons involved get entrenched in their positions and become defensive, and thus there is little chance of communication taking place. Ideally, the leader facilitates the disagreement by assisting the persons to engage in reflective listening. Sometimes the clarification of ideas solves an apparent conflict. Other times there is a real conflict which the leader facilitates in such a way that there is a possibility for compromise, so that no one is the loser. When a conflict occurs, a "win/lose" situation is more easily avoided when a specific idea is discussed instead of labeling the idea as a particular person's idea, e.g., "John's idea."

Group Phases

We often hear about encounter, sensitivity, and growth groups which emphasize personal growth and getting in touch with feelings. The two other kinds of groups which pastoral persons frequently participate in are the task-oriented group and the team-building group. The task-oriented group is formed to achieve a specific practical goal. An example of such a group is the worship committee which prepares the Sunday liturgy. A chairperson is assigned to this committee who has the function of leading the members of the committee to attain unique themes for each liturgy, and to choose appropriate music for these themes.

A team-building group is formed to develop a more closely knit group and an effective working team. These people hope to get to know each other better and to feel free to relate to each other more openly and honestly. Such a group is often composed of the members of the pastoral staff or the parish council who meet for several hours, or possibly for a couple of days at a camp in a state park, to achieve those goals.[6]

Despite the difference in goals, various groups have some common elements. In the initial stage of any group there is some orientation, hesitant participation, and a search for meaning. The members begin by introducing themselves to each other and give a little background information about themselves. The members usually hesitate to participate because they are unsure of their goal or how to attain it, and allow others to take the lead. They look to the leader for more guidance and help to begin the session. Possibly they begin speaking about the means to attain the goal, and then someone asks for a clarification of the goal of the group. A common conflict arises at this point when some of the members seek to have their social needs met, and others become anxious to begin working on the goal.

Dr. Bion, one of the early leaders of therapeutic groups for soldiers in Tavistock, England after World War II, would give no guidance to the members to the extent that sometimes initially the members weren't even sure who the leader was. He was a very passive leader who only occasionally commented on the dynamics in the group. Irvin D. Yalom believes that the leader should provide general direction to the group, yet avoid too much direction lest the group become excessively dependent on the leader. Marianne and Gerald Corey do not believe in letting the group take any direction it happens to go in. They give that amount of structure in the initial stage needed to help the members identify and express their fears, expectations, and goals. Some group leaders rigidly adhere to an agenda even when there is conflict in the group. If the conflict is brushed aside, the main topic generally will be addressed superficially. So until the conflict is openly discussed, the group will not be effective.

In the second stage there is usually some conflict, and often it is between the leader and the group members who come with different expectations of the leader of the group. Some members become disappointed in the leader because she/he is not the traditional authoritarian leader, who provides answers and solutions to questions and issues. Instead the leader urges the group to explore and use its own resources to attain the stated goal. Some members become angry at this. Since the leader is not leading authoritatively, others in their impatience try to assume the leadership role in an attempt to "get something accomplished." Sometimes this causes feelings of irritation among other members who object to the unassigned leaders becoming leaders. Friction toward the leader often occurs when the members realize they are not the leader's favorite.

The third stage of development in the group is cohesiveness. Now that the conflicts are generally over, the group gradually develops into a cohesive unit. There is an increase in morale, mutual trust, and self-disclosure. The members no longer are holding back their disagreements, but feel secure enough to voice them in the group without fear of being rejected for offering a divergent view.

In this stage the members at times unite to such an extent that they organize themselves against the rest of the world to attain their goal. To do this, they suppress all expression of negative feelings toward one another.[7]

The final phase of group development is the group-centered, productive phase. In this stage the members are concerned about each other and about working together as a group, but not to the extent that they ignore or gloss over conflicts in order to achieve harmony. The members have learned to face conflict and to use it creatively. They have also developed a greater tolerance for differences in values and behaviors, and have learned to use these effectively rather than allowing them to interfere with their work. They are aware of the dynamics in the group, and the leader's intervention is less frequent than in the initial stages. The members have learned to take the initiative rather than needing to be invited into the group interaction. Since the members take more responsibility for the effectiveness of the group, there is some sharing of the leadership with the members. This does not mean that the members become co-leaders of the group, but they initiate more interaction with others without the leader having to invite them and offer personal feedback to others. In general, they have accepted responsibility to attain a goal and now work together to do that. It should be noted that the developmental stages of groups are rarely well demarcated and that there is considerable overlap between one stage and another, and that not all groups follow in this order.[8]

In the group interaction described at the beginning of the chapter, some elements of the first two phases were present. There was some hesitation to begin the discussion, and this stage was followed by conflict.

The different phases of groups were evident in two other groups in which I was present. I was asked to be a member of the energy committee of the hospital because of my concern for energy conservation. I went to the first meeting with high expectations of accomplishing a great deal, and was frustrated when we did so little. We spent time socializing for the first several minutes. Then the chairperson called the meeting to order, stating the task

the committee was given by the administrative council, and inform-
ing the group of the limitations of its power — it could make rec-
ommendations, but not set policies. Her introductory comments
were followed by silence. As a group, we didn't know where to
begin, we didn't know what aspect of the vast energy problem should
receive our attention first. I remember leaving that room after 60
minutes, feeling very disappointed and saying to myself: "This is
going to take forever. We didn't accomplish much." The administrator of the hospital asked me later how things went in the meeting and when I shared my frustration, he said, "Well, that's what I
usually expect from any first meeting. It takes time for the group to
get to know each other before they can begin to work." This meeting illustrated the first phase of groups — hesitant participation and
orientation.

   In another group I was leading, I was reminded of all the phases
of groups. This was a Professional Advisory Group who were giving me advice concerning my Clinical Pastoral Education program.
In the first meeting, after answering a number of questions and giving some explanations about pastoral education, I stated how the
members of the group could help me achieve my goal, and a discussion ensued. Then in the middle of the second meeting, one
member surprised me by asking, "Is this what we are supposed to
do in this group?" The person needed the goal of the group re-
stated to make sure we were moving in the right direction. At this
point, I realized we were still in the first phase, "getting oriented."
After the second meeting, two members privately asked how I
thought the meetings were going. I commented that they were going
pretty well, but I hoped to move a little faster in the future. Those
members immediately agreed, and said we were getting bogged
down in details. Underneath their comments, there seemed to be
some irritation with me as a leader because I permitted the group
to move so slowly. This illustrated the second phase of the group
dynamics, some conflict. In the third and fourth meetings, I experienced the group as being a cohesive unit working on the stated goal
of helping me improve the Clinical Pastoral Education program and
at the same time acknowledging differences. This group probably

moved faster than others, because the members generally knew each other for five years before becoming members of this committee.

Group Size

The larger any group is, the less the members experience direct involvement and participation. Instead of interacting with one another, the persons often interact with the chairperson and this makes the leader very powerful. At the same time, the meeting tends to be merely an opportunity for the chairperson to give information to the others present, rather than an opportunity of engaging in real discussion. If there is to be a discussion, then the group must be small enough so each person has the opportunity to have the floor, to feel comfortable enough to express ideas and feelings, to interact meaningfully with the other members, and to obtain feedback from them.

In recent years many committees and groups of various kinds have sprung up in churches. In the beginning, since there was a tremendous effort to have every person adequately represented, the groups were usually very large. One diocesan group had 42 members, which caused a great deal of frustration and anger because there was no room for discussion or spontaneity. In addition, it took too long to have something placed on the agenda, and few results could be seen from the expenditure of so much time and energy. Then the bishop reduced the group to 24 which was helpful, but the members still found that it was too large to achieve their goals. So they reduced it to 15, and now find the group more effective because there is ample opportunity for interaction with all the participants.

In a counseling group or an interpersonal-relations group (as is present in Clinical Pastoral Education programs), generally fewer members are present than in task-oriented groups such as a committee to determine the clergy's salary. This is necessary to allow for more interaction among the members. Some years ago in a large C.P.E. center, three supervisors led one large interpersonal group in which there were 15 students. In such a large group it was impossible for some members to receive adequate attention. It took more courage to request time and receive feedback, and enabled some silent members to be observers, without ever being invited to share in the group. Some members benefited very little from that group experience. Many leaders of these interpersonal groups feel that four to eight participants is an ideal, while twice that number is acceptable in church councils or committees (task-oriented groups).[9]

Group Norms

The establishment of certain norms for a group is helpful so that group cohesion is attained. The participants need to know what is expected and what kind of behavior is acceptable in the group. These norms can be formal or informal, explicit or implicit. If the norms are to be effective, the members need to be aware of them and need to be willing to accept them. Obviously, members are likely to accept those standards which they understand and the ones in which they have had a part in selecting. For this reason, it is wise for the leader to avoid imposing norms on the group autocratically without discussion.

Some norms that have proved helpful to some groups are the following:

1. Members are expected to attend regularly and be present on time. When the members attend sessions only sporadically, the entire group suffers. Besides, members who attend regularly may resent the lack of commitment on the part of those who frequently miss meetings.
2. Participants are expected to come to the meetings prepared to discuss the issues on the agenda and to do the appropriate reading and reflecting before the meeting begins.
3. Members are urged to participate freely during the meet-

ings, sharing their opinions and feelings as they arise. In this way the group will fully benefit from their experience and skill, and the best possible decision will be made.

4. Members are expected to give feedback to one another. It is helpful in attaining the goals of the group if the members share their perceptions and reactions.

Possibly another norm to be discussed is that of confidentiality. However, these are only examples and the important issue is that the norms be discussed and accepted by all the members. Many groups fail to achieve their goal because members are unsure what is expected of them and don't know what the norms are.[10]

Group Pairing

When pairing occurs in a group, this needs to be analyzed. Sometimes it is a method that persons employ to get into a group when they are fearful of becoming active by themselves. These people chime in to agree with what another person has said and because of this participation, they feel part of the group. Later on, these persons feel comfortable enough to participate more fully, and possibly have enough courage to disagree with someone or introduce a new idea. On the other hand, the pairing of two persons in constant disagreement usually means something entirely different. Sometimes it means they are expressing the sentiments of the whole group — all the members are angry, but prefer to sit on the sidelines and have their anger expressed indirectly through the angry pair. At other times, it means that the rest of the members don't want to work toward their stated goal and so they encourage, or at least tolerate, the pair engaging in continued fruitless fighting.

If the members allow pairing to continue for an extended period of time, it could mean that they are looking upon the pair as an expression of hope that from their union the group will be saved and all the group's goals will be attained. After people struggle for some time to arrive at suitable solutions and only meet with failure, they eagerly look to two united members for hope that somehow through them success will be achieved.[11] Finally the pairing could mean that two members have had a pre-group meeting and determined to work together toward a definite goal. This type of pairing is comparable to the "ramrod" method mentioned earlier. This puts the other members at an extreme disadvantage and has a disruptive effect. If any grouping occurs outside the regular group, it is only fair that it be reported to all the members at the next meeting so that conspiracy is avoided.[12]

Dangers

In any group there are certain dangers. First, there is the danger of an attitude of "don't rock the boat." This causes the members to reach a decision without really discussing all the alternatives. Everyone secretly agrees to be nice, and individuals feel social pressure to arrive at a quick solution. As a result, they do not voice any disagreement, permitting any decision to be approved. In this type of discussion, the members short circuit the group process in order to arrive at an easy decision.

A second danger to be aware of is the "bandwagon" effect. Sometimes, it happens that the first one or two speakers are very articulate and so convincingly express their ideas that they have a snowball effect on the group. Others support their ideas totally, and again there is no disagreement. Social pressure is also present to continue agreeing with each other, rather than exploring all the possibilities. When this occurs, the leader might openly ask for any opposing views. It might be that there are none, but at least this kind of statement by the leader encourages other opinions to be expressed. In the sample interaction with the nurses in labor and delivery, this snowballing effect seems to have occurred. Once the three vocal and upset nurses shared their opinions and feelings, it seemed that no one had the courage to disagree with them. In a similar meeting with the nurses on the afternoon shift, one nurse initially agreed with the idea of the inappropriateness of baptizing dead babies. However, when a number of nurses immediately disagreed with her and strongly supported the old custom of baptizing all fetuses and stillborn infants, she felt strongly outnumbered and feared to disagree with the rest of the nurses with whom she worked every day. She did not voice any opinion during the rest of the meeting, nor did anyone support her.   .

Naturally, there is a danger of one person dominating the discussion. This means that one person is allowed to have a great share of time during the meeting, with little time left for other persons to voice their ideas. This kind of person defeats the purpose of group discussion, namely, seeking many viewpoints from many different people. Group pressure needs to be brought about so others have a chance to participate. Sometimes the leader monopolizes the discussion and doesn't allow others to become involved in the decision-making process. This happened in one church council where some laymen responded by resigning because they were angry that the supposed shared responsibility of the church council was simply a farce.

A fourth danger is to allow the discussion to develop into a heated argument so that the parties involved spend all their efforts in winning their viewpoint rather than in making the best decision.

A fifth danger is to assume that one person speaks for the whole group. This might occur when a very vocal person expresses an opinion with great emotion, or when silence follows. Since no one is voicing a different idea, the leader is tempted to presume that one person has spoken for the whole group. This might be true, but it could be that others have different ideas and need a little encouragement to share them. It is helpful in these circumstances for the leader to wonder aloud if anyone else has another idea on the topic.

In one group which I led, a participant loudly and dogmatically shared his ideas on how groups ought to be conducted, and at the same time angrily criticized my method of leading the group.

Since his opinion was followed by silence, unfortunately I presumed the whole group felt this way and immediately began defending my manner of leading the group. My defensiveness only caused the entire situation to become hopeless. Later one member came to me privately and commented how she liked the way I led the group.

A final danger lies in hidden agendas which hinder the group process and prevent the group from working on their expressed goals. People come to groups for many reasons in addition to the expressed purpose of the meeting. Some come to meet their own needs as well as attain the goal of the group. This is a fact of life and is neither good or bad, right or wrong. Problems arise when an individual's own needs inhibit the group from attaining its goal. These needs may be social or emotional, known or unknown, but they are there. So every group is working on two levels, the expressed goals of the group and the unspoken goals of the members. If these hidden agendas interfere with the group's functioning, the leader assists the group to handle the issues by bringing them to the surface and dealing with them openly. They need to be recognized and worked out. This does not mean they are necessarily dealt with immediately, because the members might openly decide to wait until later to handle them.

A good example of hidden agendas occurred in a discussion group where it was clearly stated that the members were to read a chapter of the book each month before the meeting so that it could be discussed. All the members were given copies of the book well in advance, so that they had ample time to read the first chapter. After the opening prayer of the first meeting, everyone looked at the pastor to lead the group even though another person was appointed the chairperson. When the pastor did not initiate any discussion, the chairperson began to lead by giving some background material for the book, and tried to get a discussion started by asking a couple of simple questions. However, the members responded to the questions with very brief answers or silence. The leader tried again to get some discussion started but failed. During the periods of silence, everyone looked at the pastor for some help and when he did not give any, the members felt betrayed. Why did he just sit there and leave them to struggle so much? Needless to say, the members began feeling very helpless, and became angry at their pastor for not initiating some attempts to prevent the group from becoming a total failure. Finally, the chairperson turned to the pastor and openly pleaded for help. Instead of answering their questions and helping to initiate any discussion, he asked simply what they expected of him. One by one they gradually admitted they expected him to do a great deal of teaching, so that it was necessary for them only to skim over the chapter a few minutes before the group began. So their "hidden agenda" was that the pastor would do most of the work. The chairperson thought for sure that the pastor would help him by asking better questions than he formulated, so that the group would begin to function. The agenda of the pastor was to be an observer, and so he walked into the meeting determined to say very little during the meeting. Obviously, the hidden agendas of the different people had to be dealt with before anything could be accomplished.

An Example of a Church Group

I will present a fictitious role-playing situation to illustrate some points concerning groups.[13] The education commission appointed a committee to investigate an appropriate text to be used for the grade school children in the religion class. For years the children have been using one of the catechisms which came out shortly after the Second Vatican Council. Now, with the introduction of the new *Catechism of the Catholic Church*, many feel there needs to be a change so that a more modern text is used which integrates the teachings of the new *Catechism* with the benefits of modern psychology and some new and innovative teaching techniques. The members of the education committee are meeting on Monday evening at 7:30 in the basement of the rectory. They are seated in the following manner:

Mr. Robert Rules
(chairperson)

Rev. Pete Smith	Mrs. Constance Law
(pastor)	(An interested mother)
Miss Beth Withit	Mrs. Virginia Schmidt
(director of religious education)	(An interested mother)
Miss Mary Modern	Mrs. Dolorita Depress
(A new teacher)	(A veteran teacher)
Miss Victoria Fox	Mr. Ford Sheckles
(A veteran teacher)	(finance chairperson)
Miss Sally Smiles	Mr. George Truth
(teenage representative)	(parish council representative)

Mr. John Fidelity
(A retired, dedicated church member)

The following takes place in the committee meeting. Mr. Robert Rules opens the meeting by asking Rev. Pete Smith to offer a prayer. Then Mr. Robert Rules asks if all the members know one another, and when they all nod, he states the purpose of the meeting — to decide on an appropriate text for the grade school children in the religion program. Mr. George Truth requests more information about the various ages of the children in the program and wants to know the present text the teachers have. The chairperson responds by saying that the children are from six to fourteen years old and presently they are using the Such-and-Such Catechism. Sally Smiles, the teenage representative, mentions that she enjoyed her classes because the teachers were nice and brought the students candy sometimes. Constance Law comments that last week's first Communion Mass for the children was simply beautiful. Victoria Fox agrees and remarks that all the children seemed to enjoy the lessons she had taught them this year. Ford Sheckles notes that all the teachers deserve the gratitude of the parish because of their diligence in preparing classes. Meanwhile Beth Withit shuffles her papers, and Virginia Schmidt wonders if it is true that the enrollment is down 10% this year. Mr. Rules states that her figures are accurate and then urges the group to get back to the topic and deal openly with the task at hand — do we think the present catechism ought to be discarded in favor of a more modern text.

The second interaction begins with Miss Beth Withit giving an emotional appeal to the group not to change the religion texts but to continue using the present books which put a needed emphasis on love and helping one's neighbor, instead of learning a lot of material the children aren't interested in. She supports her proposal with quotes from Vatican II and from the pastor. When she is finished, she nods to the pastor who becomes embarrassed and says nothing. Silence prevails in the group until Mr. Rules asks if there are any other opinions on the subject. Finally, Mrs. Virginia Schmidt speaks at length expressing her concern for the children's proper understanding of their religion and whether they know the act of contrition for their first confession. Mrs. Constance Law supports Mrs. Schmidt, pointing out the necessity for the children to know the commandments of God, the rules of their religion, and the seven sacraments of the Church. She concludes by saying that she was taught with the old *Baltimore Catechism* which contained a lot of information and it didn't hurt her one bit. Miss Fox whispers to Sally Smiles, while Dolorita Depress, John Fidelity, and George Truth stare at Mr. Rules who looks helplessly at Rev. Pete Smith.

After a moment of silence, Mary Modern initiates the third interaction by explaining how she used to fear God because of the education she received in her catechism classes which were based on the rote memorization of facts. She goes on to say how it took a charismatic prayer group to help her regard God as a loving Father rather than as a Judge. As she concludes, she looks hopefully at the pastor who finally speaks, noting that Vatican II urged the whole Church to update itself and that part of that modernization has led to the publication of the new, universal *Catechism of the*

Catholic Church. He strengthens his arguments by saying that the bishops indicated at their last national meeting that a change in catechisms is appropriate. His final comment is that something has to happen or else we will lose the youth of the parish, and that the young people seem to be seeking something solid. All the while he speaks, John Fidelity nods in agreement as does Mrs. Law and Mrs. Schmidt.

Silence reigns in the group again as the fourth interaction begins, until Mr. Rules wonders if anyone wants to make a motion since the discussion seems to be over. Mrs. Law and Mrs. Schmidt pull their chairs away from the table, Sally Smiles chews harder on her gum, John Fidelity picks at his finger nails, Mrs. Depress wipes her eyes with her handkerchief, and Mr. Sheckles clears his throat nervously asking if it is proper for anyone to make a motion before there is some discussion on how much it would cost to replace the present catechisms.

The fifth interaction begins when Mrs. Law and Mrs. Schmidt together complain how much damage the changes have done to the Church, and how necessary it is to get back to teaching something more substantial than "love, love, love." Miss Withit and Miss Modern interrupt, echoing their sentiments again, only louder this time. The pastor looks up at the ceiling, while Miss Fox smiles cunningly as each person speaks, and Mr. Fidelity continues his quiet efforts to listen to all the ideas expressed. Finally, Mr. Rules pounds the table with his gavel and requests that before persons speak they be recognized by the chair. After twenty more minutes of arguing, Mr. Truth makes a motion that they investigate the matter more thoroughly so a more agreeable solution can be achieved. The members readily agree that nothing can be settled at this time, and the meeting comes to an end.

The readers might want to pause and draw their own conclusions about this group process before I comment about each interaction. Even though the chairperson clearly states the goal of the meeting at the beginning, the members are unsure what to do. They hesitate to really tackle the issue by gathering more facts, and they talk about matters that are not relevant. Possibly they are hesitant, too, because they want to avoid a conflict which they know will result when they discuss a religion text.

In the second interaction the group moves from phase one, hesitation, to some aspects of phase two where conflict occurs. The director of religious education initiated the conflict by forcefully stating her views and by quoting the pastor as supporting her ideas. This gave others the impression that there was a collusion between her and the pastor. As a result, the other members sat there somewhat helpless until they were rescued by the chairperson, who asked if there were any divergent viewpoints. This helped the discussion because it gave the two mothers the courage to disagree. If he hadn't intervened in this way, the discussion might have ended there, with only one viewpoint being expressed. When the conflict occurred, some of the members became angry at the chairperson for not helping them return to a pleasant conversation.

Pairing has definitely developed within the group by the third interaction. This is evident by what is said and by the seating the various members have chosen. The director of religious education and the new teacher have similar views, and so they sit together to support each other. The same is true of the two mothers. Another aspect of the seating arrangement is that the persons with opposing viewpoints sit directly opposite each other as in a chess match. Although a chairperson is assigned, the members periodically look to the pastor for help when they need assistance. In the second interaction the chairperson hoped for assistance from the pastor, and now the teacher does after she has the courage to reveal some personal aspects of her life. So the pastor is viewed as a leader even though he is not the assigned leader.

The fourth interaction began with the group involved in a heated conflict, and nobody seemed to know how to handle it. The pastor had expressed his views and supported them with quotes from important sounding sources, and so the teachers felt helpless to oppose their spiritual leader, but they clearly didn't agree. They expressed their feelings by pulling their chairs away from the others. Others displayed their anxiety by various nervous mannerisms. There was definitely an impasse.

Finally, the two teachers got enough courage to disagree openly with the pastor, and together expressed some old pains they had experienced with a content-oriented catechism. Sharing with the group some old hurts that were still very present to them, they had come to the group prepared to block any changes which would take them back, as they feared, to pre-Vatican II days. This was their hidden agenda as they came to the group. Unfortunately the meeting ended in chaos because several other persons had come to the meeting with similar hidden agendas, and there was little room for real dialogue and communication during the meeting.

Miss Fox continued throughout all the interactions playing her role of conniver. John Fidelity was the faithful Church member who is the silent observer. Mr. Rules was the structurer and the expediter even though he ultimately failed, while Miss Withit, Miss Modern, Mrs. Law, and Mrs. Schmidt alternated in being the aggressors during the meeting.

Footnotes

[1] Arthur X. Degan II, "Group Process Techniques," *Pastoral Life*, February 1971, pp. 14-15.

[2] Bruce Skaggs, "Group Supervision," *The Supervision of Pastoral Care*, David A. Steere, Ed., Westminister/John Knox Press, Louisville, KY, 1989, p. 178.

[3] Arthur X. Degan II, "The Priest and Group Decision Making," *Pastoral Life*, January 1971, pp. 18-21.

[4] Irvin D. Yalom, *The Theory and Practice of Group Psychotherapy*, Basic Books Inc., New York, NY, 1975, p. 477.

[5] Gerald Corey and Marianne Schneider Corey, *Groups: Process and Practice*, Brooks-Cole Publishing Co., Monterey, CA, 1977, pp. 41-42.

[6] Carl Rogers, *On Encounter Groups*, Harper and Row Publishers, New York, NY, 1970, p. 5.

[7] Irvin D. Yalom, *op. cit.*, pp. 303-312.

[8] Merle M. Ohlsen, *Group Counseling*, Holt, Rinehart and Winston Inc., New York, NY, 1970, p. 59.

[9] Merle M. Ohlsen, *op. cit.*, p. 58.

[10] Gerald Corey and Marianne Schneider Corey, *op. cit.*, p. 23.

[11] W.R. Bion, *Experience in Groups*, Ballantine Books, New York, NY, 1978, 3rd Printing, pp. 135-137.

[12] Irvin D. Yalom, *op. cit.*, p. 339.

[13] Richard A. Donnenwirth, "An Experience in Groups," an unpublished paper, Bethesda Hospital, Cincinnati, OH, 1978.

CHAPTER NINE

RELATING ERIKSON'S STAGES TO THEOLOGY AND MINISTRY

I N MY OWN LIFE, I HAVE RECENTLY noticed certain themes recurring. Several years ago I changed positions as chaplain, moving from a 330-bed hospital to a 750-bed hospital. Reflecting on that experience, I remember that initially in my anxiety in a new setting, I had trouble "giving" to the patients and the personnel because I wanted "to get" something before giving. After I experienced receiving some support from the personnel, I was able to give to them. Further, I observed that after the sick received love and acceptance from me, they were able to give themselves in trust to my care. So I noticed the theme of "getting and giving in return." (I wish to credit Rev. Richard A. Donnenwirth of Bethesda Hospital in Cincinnati, Ohio for the seminal thoughts present in this chapter.)

During my years at my present position, I have made a number of changes in the Pastoral Care Department, expanding it and seeking to hire certified chaplains. I have incorporated in the department most of my original goals, and now realize I accept suggestions concerning changes in the department with reluctance because my tendency is to be very cautious to maintain what I have brought into existence. This represents another theme occurring in my life, "to make be and to take care of."

In preparation for certification as a supervisor in the Association of Clinical Pastoral Education, I studied Dr. Erik Erikson. After his study of Sigmund Freud and his work with many men and women as a psychiatrist, he concluded that human beings pass through eight stages from birth to death. Erikson notes in his book, *Childhood and Society* that themes from all these stages periodically recur in our lives.[1] His ideas were of interest to me because they helped me attain a better understanding of life in general and in particular, gain insights about my own recent experiences. The themes from his stages made sense, too, as I studied my interactions with patients who enacted these themes under the stress of illness. Experience indicates that in all our lives there are major themes which reoccur. This is true in my life as a pastoral care person, as well as in the life of the sick. In ministering, I discovered the importance of noting the themes that appear in the life of the sick person, as well as being aware of the major theme occurring in my life. In this way, I make use of myself in helping others.

It is my hope that the following ideas will bring greater understanding to lay, religious and ordained ministers of themselves as persons and of the people to whom they minister. I explain Dr. Erikson's eight stages, describing each one of them with its mode of behavior and its developmental task. Next, I integrate this stage of theme of life with theology, often receiving assistance to do this from the book, *Growing Up to God*.[2] Finally, I apply this to sick persons who exhibit some of these themes during their illness.

First Stage

In the first stage the behavioral mode is "to get and to give in return." In this stage, which exists from birth until the child is one year old, the infant is frequently seeking to satisfy his needs. He wants to be loved, to be fed, to be changed, etc. He learns to give something in return too, e.g., a smile. If the infant successfully works through his behavior, learning to get and to give, then he begins to trust people. For example, when mommy and daddy leave the home to go to a movie, the infant trusts they will return and not abandon him. In addition to learning to trust his parents and other significant people in his life, the infant struggles to trust himself because as an infant he doesn't earn love or care from his parents. So the developmental task in this period of the infant's life is basic "trust vs. mistrust."

From a theological perspective, this period is "unmerited grace" because God loves the infant just as it is. He loves us first while we are unworthy of his love, and we respond to that love by loving him in return. We demonstrate our love by worshipping God. Continuing on the theological plane, the issue of "trust vs. mistrust" is reflected in our attitude toward God. Do we trust God as a loving Creator, or do we fear him and become anxious at the thought of being in his presence? The Bible extols fear of God, but when it does, it refers to fear in the sense of respect and obedience rather than of anxiety which creates a distance between ourselves and God.[3]

When people become sick, they come to the hospital "to get well" and give themselves, in a sense, to the medical team to diagnose the cause of the illness and to cure it. For example, to be freed from headaches a person gives up his regular schedule and undergoes the discomfort of many tests to determine its cause. Another patient is willing to give up his gangrenous limb in order to save his life, and another undergoes the removal of a cancerous kidney to live several more years.

In this stage, there is also a generalized fear of the unfamiliar — of the large hospital with its many tests and its medical terms which are like a foreign language to most patients. This likewise raises the issue of "trust vs. mistrust." It takes time for the patient to trust the chaplain. Often rapport must be established before the patient lets the chaplain enter his inner world. If the patient has experienced a lot of trust in life, the rapport and trust occur easily. However, if the patient suffers from a lack of trust, there is likely to be little rapport established in the patient-chaplain relationship.

Second Stage

The second stage of life is "to hold on and to let go" and is comparable to Freud's anal stage — the holding on and letting go of waste matter. This period, which lasts from ages one to three, enables a child to learn what is his property, his body, and what belongs to others. In other words, an understanding of self and others gradually evolves. Normally, in an attempt to attain some autonomy, the child engages in rebellion. Connected with this struggle, the child realizes there is a lack of control, a lack of knowing what is hers and what is somebody else's. When a child is caught taking her neighbor's new bike without asking permission to see how much better it is than her own, she feels shame and doubt. So the developmental task at this point is "autonomy or self-control vs. shame and doubt."

Theologically, this stage is comparable to the account in the Garden of Eden where Adam and Eve failed to act on the distinction between what is God's (the tree of the knowledge of good and evil) and what is theirs (every other tree in the garden). They could eat of all the trees except the one which God did not want them to touch. But they couldn't resist the temptation and took the fruit of the tree and ate it anyway. As a result of their failure, they felt shame (they realized their nakedness) which raises the issue for us of self-control over our bodies and their functions. Connected with this account is the temptation of the devil who urged Adam and Eve to eat the fruit of the forbidden tree in order to become like God. This aspect illustrates the struggle to understand who we are (what is self) and who God is (what is other than self). So it is also the stage of personhood where we struggle to a limited extent to determine who we are and who the other person is.

Sick persons experience some difficulty continuing to value themselves because they are no longer in complete control. As a result, they begin to doubt their worth and feel shame. If a sick person is extremely insecure, control of her life probably is important to her and, as a result, she struggles with the tension of how much control to give the medical team. If she is a business executive, having a great deal of control over other people's jobs and lives, then she often finds it difficult to be controlled by another, e.g., the nurse enforcing the doctor's order. Thus, control is a basic issue with sick persons too.

In particular, stroke victims and those suffering from spinal cord injuries and cardiac problems experience doubt and shame because of the limitations their sickness places upon them. Cardiac patients might have more problems than others because externally they seem so healthy. Pastoral persons, in ministering to these people, do not blame them for their illness, but rather accept them realizing that their illness, with its limitations, is a loss which causes the person to grieve. Ministers support them in their grief and emphasize what the patients can still do, even though they are limited in some way. With the patient who loses her fingers in an accident, it's beneficial to be with her in her pain of adjusting. Pastoral persons speak with her in her shame as she gradually lets go of the functions she can no longer perform, and as she holds on to the functions she can still accomplish. Possibly, the ministers can help her to perfect other aspects of her personality that are underdeveloped.

Third Stage

From ages three to six, the child engages in playing house like daddy and mommy. This playacting develops her imagination and creativity, and enables her to attain sex role differentiation. During this time the child begins to learn how to deal with her aggressive and sexual feelings. Guilt results in the child when she overextends herself, and this guilt functions as a restraining force in her behavior. Erikson describes the mode of behavior of this stage as "to make and to make like" while he depicts the developmental task as "initiative vs. guilt."

Theologically, sin and redemption quickly come to mind as

related to this stage. Peter denied Our Lord three times and rightly felt guilty about his sin. Jesus came and offered him redemption when he asked him three times, "Do you love me?" This stage is associated with conscience formation when a person learns what is right and wrong. As a result of transgressing the dictates of her conscience by allowing her sexual and aggressive drives to go unrestrained, sin enters her life and she needs redemption.

Viewing this stage from the sick room, those patients come to mind whose imagination and creativity led them to dream of themselves as a movie star or president of some big company and now realize, as they lie in a hospital with a lot of time to think, that they will never attain that dream. Other patients who fit into this category are those who allowed their aggressive or sexual drives full freedom, so that they now feel very guilty about their past. Other sick persons such as heart patients who retire early because of their illness, experience this feeling of guilt too because they are not working, not doing their part in sharing family responsibilities, or because they view their sickness as causing a disruption in a normal family life.

Finally, some patients feel guilty because they think they are responsible for their illness. One lady, who fell down her stairs at home after having surgery for a new hip socket, broke her leg. She felt totally responsible for that "dumb act because I should have asked my son to help me." Pastoral persons urge such a person to express her guilt and then accept herself as she views herself. Often this acceptance helps to reduce her guilt feelings and enables her to accept herself as a sick person. At times, though, pastoral persons challenge the sick person concerning her feelings of guilt by asking questions about her responsibility for the sickness, her previous acts of responsibility for her family, etc.

Fourth Stage

Successfully passing through the first three stages of life, children acquire the strength to cope with the fourth where the behavioral mode is "to make things, and to make things together." Children make things manually and conceptually, and, at the same time, learn to cooperate with others, especially as they enter school. Beginning in kindergarten, they learn to make things with clay and to make greeting cards for their parents on Mother's and Father's Day. They learn to jump rope, form a circle, and how to play other games where cooperation with other children is necessary. Feelings of inferiority enter into a child's life when he compares himself to others, realizing he can't do some things as well as other people can. Reluctantly, a child even admits to himself occasionally that there are some things he simply can't do at all. Thus, the developmental task from ages six to twelve is "industry vs. inadequacy and inferiority."

The theology of "good works" is related to this period. We are a redeemed people because of Jesus' love for us, his death and resurrection in our behalf. He gave us faith as a free gift because of who we are, not because of what we have done. Our worth, then, comes from Jesus, and our good works flow naturally from our living faith. As James says in his epistle, "Faith without works is dead," and so good works are part of our salvation which flow from our faith.

Some sick persons emphasize this theme excessively and, because they aren't doing their normal work, feel inferior. These people have a self-image which is built on how much they produce. In other words, these persons have the motto that "worklessness equals worthlessness," and so they aren't content just "to be," but must always "be doing." Some management people especially have difficulty during illness because they have attained constant promotions through their hard work. Ministers urge persons with this kind of personality to realize that they equate work with worth, and invite them to form new criteria for determining their worth and the value of other people, especially their family members.

Fifth Stage

When a child becomes a teenager, he participates in a rite which indicates his passage into adulthood, e.g., confirmation or bar mitzvah, if he is a member of a religious group. As a young adult, he attempts to discover his new identity. He tries out different roles to see which one fits comfortably in his own attempt to know who he is. He desires to become independent and to be his own person. He tends to get an over-idealized picture of himself and the world; then he tends to become an absolute realist, the opposite of that idealism. So he vacillates frequently during this period of his life and, in addition, fights to accept his limitations as part of his own uniqueness. Thus, the behavioral mode of the fifth stage, existing from ages 13 to 15, is "to be oneself and to share oneself with others," and its developmental task is "identity vs. diffusion."

Teenagers begin to question the value system they have been taught by their parents and religious leaders, and further question the basic truths of their religion. As a result, they raise questions like: What does it mean to be fully human? What is a human being in relationship to another human being? What obligations does a person have to God as a result of his relationship? What obligations does a person have to other persons? And more specifically, what is their relationship to their parents, brothers, sisters, country? Finally, what obligations do I have to these persons? Teenagers ask these questions in an effort to be themselves and to share themselves with others.

The theme of this stage is particularly present for persons who have suffered strokes, spinal cord injuries, and mastectomies. If a young man has played on the high school football or baseball team and then suffers a spinal cord injury, he attempts to be himself again. When that fails, he tries to establish a new identity. When a woman suffers a mastectomy or stroke, she may find it very difficult to share herself sexually with her husband. Many other hospitalized persons struggle with this theme because now they view themselves as sick and so attempt to determine their identity as sick faith-filled persons, and perhaps try to be the "good patient" who conceals all their real frustrations and anger about being sick. Another tension is experienced when patients are treated as things or diseases rather than as unique persons. Pastoral persons urge the personnel to relate to the patients as unique persons. They bring this notion of uniqueness to the patients by their manner of interacting with them, and emphasize this point during orientation for new personnel and in other programs for them.

Sixth Stage

The lives of teenagers from 16 to 19 are marked by forming intimate relationships with people of both sexes. At this time a person tests how close she can get to another without losing her own identity. Two girls become almost inseparable, doing everything and going everywhere together. Steady dating with deep sharing of self too becomes the common practice. They lose themselves in a relationship with another person, only to discover later that human beings need space as well as intimacy. Normally, persons can't stand 24 hours a day of intimacy, and this is best borne out on vacation. Two of the best friends go on vacation and after ten days "of total togetherness," they realize they need distance from one another for a few hours. If a person refuses to enter into a close relationship with anyone, she becomes isolated. There is no sharing of herself with another or receiving of another in her life, and so she lives in her own world, cut off from others. Thus "to lose and to find oneself in another" is the behavioral mode while the developmental task is "intimacy and distance vs. self-absorption and isolation."

As one person draws closer to another, she opens herself to being loved and accepted, and to being criticized, hurt and rejected. In this process of drawing close to someone, it is likely that the person's ideas and values will undergo change. Thus, a teenager often changes her relationship to her parents and alters some of her values too. Naturally, this is a cause of tension between them.

Jesus exemplifies in his life this behavior of losing and finding life in another. He lost his life for us, and yet found it in giving himself out of love for us. Further, his relationship to his apostles exemplifies this behavior. For he spent much of his time teaching them, losing himself in them, and, at the same time, found himself and his mission in this interaction with them. For example, one day after he spoke at length about his kingdom, the apostles were arguing among themselves as they were walking along about who would be the greatest in that kingdom. Jesus displayed his own uniqueness at this point, clearly explaining that the greatest in his kingdom is the one who is the servant of all the rest. He also displayed his need for intimacy by being with the apostles frequently, and yet he spent some nights alone praying to his Father, and some other time relaxing with his friends, Mary, Martha, and Lazarus.

Finally, this stage exemplifies closeness and distance from God. Oftentimes, we wish that our prayer life would give us a feeling of being very intimate with God. However, in reality there are many times when we experience a certain coolness in prayer — there is no intimacy with God. Another aspect of this stage is the experience of Christian fellowship with our fellow parishioners. There is a certain oneness worshipping in the same church, and a deeper unity can result when people serve on the same committee.

In ministering to those confined to their homes or the hospital, the issue of finding and losing oneself arises in a unique manner. Ministers visit and offer their services to the sick, and generally make a contribution to the sick person's welfare. It is equally important for the clergy to realize their contribution by losing themselves in leaving the sick room. Henry Nouwen states, "In this way the memory of our visit can become as important, if not more important, then the visit itself. I am deeply convinced that there is a ministry in which our leaving creates space for God's spirit and in which, by our absence, God can become present in a new way."[4]

When sick persons are hospitalized, pastoral persons are aware that sickness causes distance in relationships, that patients feel cut off from their families and friends. So the clergy facilitates contact between them. If a person is a patient in an intensive care unit or in the emergency room, then he is likely to feel this isolation more intensely. For these patients and their families, sometimes chaplains seek to be the "conveyor" of communication so that this sense of isolation is reduced and, at other times, attempt to become "new family members" by their concerned presence. Experience also reveals that often psychiatric patients have difficulty with intimacy and isolation.

Seventh Stage

"To make be and to take care of" is the behavioral mode of the next stage while "generativity vs. stagnation" is the developmental task. During this time people pair off and marry, and from this union comes a desire to generate and to take care of the children flowing from this union. There is also a desire to generate things, to promote values in future generations, and to create one's place in life by attaining status in a particular profession. Having accomplished this, some people feel a need to care for the thing created and the values promoted, while others reduce their need to take responsibility.

Creation and co-creation with God are related to this stage from a theological perspective. We are co-creators with God of other human beings through marriage, and we further create ideas, professions, and movements through the inspiration of God and the assistance of other persons. We reflect on our obligation to take responsibility for what God has given us in his creation, e.g., the environment and clean air, and to care for what we ourselves have created.

This theme recalls those patients who have been rendered sterile from surgical procedures, e.g., hysterectomy, sterilization procedures, and severe spinal injuries. These persons come to mind because they can no longer procreate children, and pastoral persons can assist them in struggling with the issue of generativity. It's important also to consider people who are becoming elderly and, as a result, are struggling with the realization that their bodies are aging. Some senior citizens experience difficulty in generating new ideas, and even in maintaining what they have fought so long to bring into existence. For a few, the struggle is simply to maintain their own life.

Pastoral persons urge the sick and elderly to continue to create, and challenge them not to give up. One young man whose legs are paralyzed has become a social worker in a rehabilitation unit of a hospital, where he helps other people adjust to the limitations their sickness or accident has forced on them. Senior citizens are often only limited by their vision of what is possible to them. One man went back to college after he retired, because he always wanted to obtain a college degree. Others upon retiring, learned to play golf and now are proficient at it.

Eighth Stage

The final stage of Erikson's list is "to be through having been and to face not being." Here elderly persons look back, reflecting on their accomplishments and the people they have known, those they have loved, and those they have lost through death and moving. The elderly need to integrate their lives as they come to an end, and need to blend all their life together so they can see their lives as meaningful. If they cannot discover any meaning, then the elderly become disgusted and despair. Thus, their developmental task is "integrity vs. despair and disgust."

Theologically, this stage is classified as eschatology, the last things which include death and judgment, heaven and hell. During this time the elderly reexamine death and the meaning it has for them, realizing that it is approaching. It's a time, too, for them to deepen their faith in heaven where Jesus has prepared a place for them since their birth. This stage is associated with Simeon who viewed his life as complete when he saw the Christ Child. There were no regrets, no hanging on, no despair, but rather life as well as death made sense for him. He was ready to make that journey into eternity. Simeon's religious beliefs helped him integrate life and death, and such beliefs can help other people also to find meaning in life, in suffering, in aging, in dying, and in eternity.

Pastorally in this stage, ministers help geriatric patients through their remembrances to integrate their lives. Pastoral persons assist dying patients to prepare for not being. When they have put their life together, such patients find it easier to die because they feel a certain completion of their life on this earth. It's easier when they look forward to a life after death with their God because of their faith.

In ministering to the elderly and dying, pastoral persons help them to evaluate whether they can face their condition, or if they need to deceive themselves and not face reality. Rather than forcing the person to face the truth, pastoral persons seek out the reason they need to deny reality and then deal with that need. A person might need to deny his dying condition because he hasn't made his peace with God, or because there are no provisions for the care of his invalid wife.

To achieve solidarity with the sick, it is essential to know where they are coming from and where we are coming from. To be compassionate with an individual, it is helpful to understand what struggles he is experiencing and what struggles we are undergoing. Clergy are assisted in doing this by attaining some understanding of Dr. Erik Erikson's eight stages. In pastoring the sick they keep his stages or themes in the back of their mind, and bring them to their attention when a patient shares some feelings or struggles related to them in order that they can minister more effectively. In this chapter these stages of Erikson and their application to the sick have been described. The theological dimension has been added to provide the cement that unites these stages with the care of the sick.

Footnotes

[1] Erik Erikson, *Childhood and Society*, W.W. Norton & Co., New York, NY, 1963, pp. 248-273.

[2] John J. Gleason, Jr., *Growing Up To God*, Abingdon Press, New York, NY, 1975.

[3] *The Liturgy of The Hours*, Volume II, Catholic Book Publishing Co., New York, NY, 1976, pp. 185-187.

[4] Henry Nouwen, *The Living Reminder*, Seabury Press, New York, NY, 1977, p. 44.

CHAPTER TEN

SPIRITUALITY

S PIRITUALITY IS FORMING OR DEEPENING our relationship with God. A first step in forming such a relationship is an active prayer life. This is done by making a daily appointment with God and conversing with him in a manner satisfying to our unique personality. Another step is being open to the many and varied ways God speaks to us. He reveals himself to us as we develop our sexual, emotional, intellectual, bodily, and moral aspects. All of these aspects are you and I — elements comprising our personhood. Further, our spirituality is fashioned by how we perceive God individually and collectively as members of the human race. It involves getting in touch with our identity and others as people created in the image of God and as a revelation of God through our embodied persons. If we are crippled in any of these areas, then all the others are hampered as well, including our ability to relate to God.

This conclusion is based on my belief that wholeness and holiness are the same. As we become more whole persons, more developed and integrated, then we are becoming more holy, more like our God.[1]

St. Peter is an excellent example of one who became holy as he became more whole. Peter generally appears to be a leader, strong, in control, loyal, sincere, and a hardworking fisherman with a clear macho personality. But Peter had his shadow side too, those aspects of his personality which he found unacceptable. It seems that Peter repressed his fear of weakness and insecurity. Peter had a need for power, prestige, and authority to overcome his feelings of helplessness, weakness, and vulnerability.

One of Peter's great moments in the Gospels occurs as he fearlessly accepts Jesus' invitation to follow him after one of his failed fishing trips. Another significant moment occurred at Caesarea Philippi as he professed faith in Jesus as "the Christ, the Son of the living God." However, because Peter was out of touch with his shadow, it overcomes him when Jesus predicts his suffering and death. Here Peter projects his own weakness and fear onto Jesus saying, "Heaven preserve you, Lord; this must never happen to you" (Mt 16:22). Peter was attempting to stop Jesus on his journey to wholeness by not recognizing his own fears of loss and pain.

Later, when Jesus confronts his apostles about their lack of faith as his hour of passion approaches, Peter cannot admit even the possibility of his fear and weakness under pressure. He says, "Even if all lose faith, I will not" (Mk 14:30). When Jesus continues by predicting that Peter would deny him three times, Peter strengthened his defense mechanisms by saying, "If I have to die with you, I will never disown you" (Mk 14:31). Peter's failure to embrace his weak and fearful shadow leads to his downfall. It leads him to deny his friendship with Jesus, even to the point of denying knowing Jesus. If Peter had embraced his shadow and become more whole, probably his denial would not have occurred.[2]

To develop a spiritual life, it is necessary to know who we are, but as we struggle to discover who we are, we are confronted with the question — who is God for us? The image we have of ourselves and the image we have of God are intertwined. And often associated with both of these images is our attitude toward joy and pain as well as toward guilt and sin. If we view God as extremely demanding, then we probably perceive ourselves as great sinners, deserving of pain and punishment. If we look upon God as a person who wants total obedience, it is unlikely that we can really feel happy about enjoying life. If we have a poor image of ourselves, then pain and suffering are due to us as part of our lot in life. If we regard God as harsh and punitive, we tend to think very poorly of ourselves. If we can only be valuable, lovable when we are perfect, it's difficult for us to see ourselves as being very lovable. If we are only valuable when we are working or producing, it's difficult for us to have fun without feeling guilty. On the other hand, if we view God as a person who loves us with our strengths as well as our weaknesses, we tend to value ourselves more highly, tend to enjoy life. If we have an image of God as a merciful Father who forgives our sins as he did the Prodigal Son, it enables us to relax and be acceptable without being perfect. If we look upon God, not as some mighty Being who created the world and then lives far away from his creatures, but as someone who is with us in our daily lives, it's easy for us to feel supported and not alone in the struggles of everyday living.[3]

Biblical Images of God

God's love for us is specified in detail by John when he describes Jesus' discourse on the night before he died. There Jesus prays, asking his Father "that you love them as you loved me... so that your love for me may live in them" (Jn 17:23-26). It seems incredible but this is Jesus' prayer for us, that God the Father might love us as he loves Jesus. This is difficult for us to fathom because we would like to express God's love in degrees. We view God as loving holy people 90% and good people 70%, mediocre people 40%, halfhearted people 20% and sinners 5%. This is the way we often love others; our close friends receive more than those we don't get along with very well. It's not that way with God. God cannot possibly give 100% of his love to his Son and 70% to us. He would simply not be God if that were possible. God can only give 100% of his love to everyone. Some of the dialogues of St. Catherine of Siena with God give the impression that God is giving her his undivided attention; she perceives God totally 100% interested in everything she has to say. This is accurate because God gave his undivided attention to her just as he is willing to give it to us.[4]

In Sacred Scripture, God revealed his covenant wherein he pledges himself to be faithful to us forever despite our sinfulness and ingratitude. He said, "If they violate my statutes and keep not my commands, I will punish their crime with a rod and their guilt with stripes. Yet my kindness I will not take from them, nor will I belie my faithfulness. I will not violate my covenant; the promise of my lips I will not alter" (Ps 89:32-35). This covenant urges us to look upon God as a faithful Creator in all circumstances and evokes within us a response of adoration and humility, an awareness of God's presence in our lives. This leads us to an awareness of who we are, not what we have done or have not done. God's goodness calls forth in us an attitude of acceptance of our state of creatureliness. This experience of the all-good God enables us not only to have a deeper awareness of the absolute fidelity of God, but also of his total acceptance of us as we are.

As we place ourselves in God's presence, we are before the One who is our Creator. We feel comfortable enough to place ourselves in his presence because we realize he has loved us before the world was created. We realize that we are not the result of fate or chance, but unique persons called into existence by the creative act of God's free love. We exist because God wants us, because God loved us enough to create us. The simple truth that God freely created us indicates that God is Love in his essence and also in our behalf. Thus, even before we approach him, God has accepted and loved us as we are. Since we ourselves have changes in our mood periodically, and at times vacillate in our love toward one another, we imagine God does the same thing. We tend to project our own changeability onto our Creator. However, he is constant in his love for us just as he is constantly creating the world in which we live. He is not spying on us, waiting to catch us in our sin that he might withdraw his love from us. On the contrary, he loves us totally without reservation and wishes nothing more than that we might freely choose to return his love.

The thought of our lovableness in the eyes of God is illustrated by the way that Jesus taught us to pray. The disciples frequently watched Jesus pray and were curious how he prayed, so they asked him, "What do you say when you pray?" Jesus responded that he prayed in this manner, "Our Father..." and he gave us the privilege of addressing God as Father, too. It is truly a privilege to address God as Father. Jesus, the only begotten Son of God, had this right and he desires us to regard God as *Abba*, Father or Daddy. This invitation of Jesus to address God on such familiar terms is not only another sign of God's love for us, but it reveals to us something about the Father's personality. It reveals his kindness, love, and mercy — a desire that we approach him on the same intimate and familiar terms as Jesus himself did.

Our patriarchal tradition has generally ignored the implications of God as mother. However, the Scriptures depict God on some occasions as a mother. Here are some examples:

> "But now, I cry out as a woman in labor, gasping and panting" (Is 42:14).

> "For thus says the Lord: ... As a nursling, you shall be carried in her arms, fondled on her lap; as a mother comforts her son, so will I comfort you" (Is 66:12, 13).

> "O Jerusalem, Jerusalem, you kill the prophets and stone those who are sent to you. How often would I have gathered your children together as a hen gathers her brood under her wings, but you would not!" (Lk 13:34).

Our relationship with God is incomplete if it fails to incorporate God's motherly characteristics of tenderness, nurturing, gentleness, and creativity. God is truly the Father and Mother of nature; Jesus is truly a man who has integrated into his person his masculine and feminine characteristics. Our relationship to God needs to reflect that reality.[5]

As we try to approach God, we often struggle to express acts of love because we are not sure he is interested in hearing them. As we attempt to express our love, it is important to realize that our love for God is not as significant as his love for us. Our love for God is secondary; God's love for us is primary: "Love, then, consists in this: not that we have loved God, but that he has loved us and has sent his Son as an offering for our sins" (1 Jn 4:10).

This love God has for us is the fulfillment of a dream, because we all hope to have a friend who knows everything about us and still accepts us. We dream to meet a person with whom we can really share ourselves, a person who understands our weaknesses and loves us with these shortcomings. God is such a person because he loves us with our hopes and disappointments, our joys and our sorrows, our successes and our failures, our sacrifices and our selfishness. It is easy for us intellectually to accept the fact that God loves us; after all, that is what we have been told since grade school. Yet it is quite different to believe this on the "gut level." It takes a long time to believe I am accepted and loved by God as I am, because first we struggle to *accept* ourselves as we are and so we find it difficult to *love* ourselves as we are. We know we don't always achieve the ideal, make wrong choices, fail to achieve our goals because our talents are limited. Most of us tend to be more demanding of ourselves than God is, tend to have higher expectations of ourselves than God does, tend to be able to accept and love ourselves only if we are perfect. However, God accepts us where we are in our own individual lives, not as we should be. He loves us as we hope for healing in a particular area. Generally, this takes the experience of being accepted and loved by another human being.[6]

Secondly, we struggle to acknowledge God's acceptance and love because it demands the ability to trust. Spiritually, trust means standing on the roof of our home and hearing God say to us, "Jump and I'll catch you." The person who responds to that invitation has trust. In Erikson's eight stages of life, he lists as the first stage trust vs. mistrust. In our interpersonal relationships with other human beings, it is necessary for us to experience trust from others. It is necessary too for us to trust other people. Once we have trusted a human being, we can put our faith and trust in God whom we do not see. Obviously, this refers to St. John's statement that we cannot love God whom we do not see, if we cannot love our neighbor whom we do see.[7]

Therefore, the basis of our faith in God is our willingness to acknowledge our Creator's acceptance of us; it is allowing God to come into our lives. John said this in his epistle, "We have come to

know and to believe in the love God has for us" (1 Jn 4:16). This is
the content of all belief in God — God's love toward us. If we examine the Apostle's Creed, we discover that it is nothing more than
a statement of our belief in the love which God has for us. Twelve
times in the Creed, we express in different ways the fact that God
loves us.

Discovering Our Image of God

It is beneficial to understand the ideal image of God. It is helpful
to know who God is for our pastor, our spiritual director, and the
author of some spiritual book we value highly. However, the important issue really is who is God in our hearts. Oftentimes our
concept of God is best illustrated when a person asks us very point-
edly, "When you think of God, what do you think of? A judge who
can condemn you to hell, a critic, someone who is aloof, punitive,
stern, warm, a friend, nurturing mother, kindly father, well-wisher,
savior, or Good Shepherd?" That one word or those few words give
us a good insight into our concept of God. If God is a severe judge
or a stern father for us, then it is not likely we want to get too close
to him; we do not want to form a close relationship with him because we fear him too much. On the other hand, if God is a loving
savior or a merciful father, then we are eager to form a deep relationship. We are not afraid of him, but enjoy being in his presence.

One teacher assisted his students in gaining a deeper appreciation of their concept of God by showing one reel of three different films which portray God differently. First, he showed a reel of
Cecil B. DeMille's *The Ten Commandments* where God is aloof,
stern, and punitive. God frightened the people with his might, his
thunder and lightning, and so they feared coming near him. They
told Moses to bring God's messages to them. This was followed by
a reel from *Going My Way* in which Barry Fitzgerald played the
part of the pastor. Here God is not only extremely distant, but often doesn't seem too interested in us. He is too busy. Yet we can
attract his attention if we do something perfect and these perfect

acts win for us God's smiling approval. So our acceptance often seems based on our works. Finally, the students saw part of *Oh, God!* where God is depicted as readily available, constantly interacting with us, and supporting us, but not to the extent that we become excessively dependent upon him. After the teacher showed the films, he asked his students to write the different concepts of God that were depicted and then to identify the one that most closely matched their own.[8]

Another approach in discovering God's identity for us is to examine two different concepts of God. One concept regards him as a person who loves those who perform well. This places a tremendous obligation on our part to live exactly all the demands of the Gospel. A second view of God is not to ground our security in our performance, but rather in the good news of God's love for us. Here we strive constantly to keep in mind his radical love for us no matter what we do, and his demand that we love him, our neighbor, and ourselves. This second view regards Jesus as an outpouring of God's love for us; Jesus is God's gift to us. Because we take God's love for us so seriously, there is an urgent, radical need to respond. Because we believe in the incredibly generous gift the Creator has bestowed upon us, we have the radical demands of the Gospel.

While in the first concept we understand God's attitude toward us to vary according to our performance, in the second we simply hear the Father inviting us to love him in return for his love of us. We wonder how this can be, because our experience in life is that people are loved because of their performance. In our society we come to anticipate that others will treat us as we treat them. However, this is exactly what the good news is all about — God's ways are not our ways. God initiates his love for us and does not simply react to our performance. God so loves us that he sent his Son, who in turn so loved us, that he gave his life for us. As Jesus was about to leave us, he loved us so much that he gave us the Holy Spirit to stay with us, to give us strength and courage and to transform our hearts and lives that we might continue to do the work begun by Jesus.

Jesus knew the Creator was a loving God no matter what happened to him. He knew that his Father would take care of him because he was his Son. Jesus' security did not rest on performance, saying in effect, "All is well because I perform well." Rather, his security rested in the deep realization of his Father's love in their interpersonal relationship. Jesus stated, "The Father and I are one" (John 14:9). Their relationship was one expressed eloquently in the word Jesus prayed often: "*Abba*" which expresses their tender union. At the same time, his security was not such that he thought he would never experience loneliness or fear. He had no contract with his *Abba* that he would be protected from all harm. He had no assurance that he would only meet success and that people would always acclaim him, that he would never taste defeat, sorrow, or pain, that he would never encounter indifference, enmity, betrayal, rejection, or death. But rather, Jesus had the assurance that even in all of these, his *Abba*'s love was strong enough to support him. His security was born of love, not on how well he performed.[9]

Because of our patriarchal culture, some women need to enhance their relationship with God by searching the Scriptures for female role models. I am not suggesting Deborah who functioned as a judge, or Judith who cut off the head of an enemy general, because they became heroines by performing traditionally masculine roles. Nor would I suggest Esther who by her exquisite beauty fulfills a male ideal of femininity.

Some women have been assisted by role models like Hagar and Leah. Hagar's spirituality differs from men's in four fundamental ways: first, she begins in a position of weakness, not strength; second, she is thrust out by Abraham and Sarah into the wilderness and clearly did not choose it; third, she focuses away from herself, onto her child; fourth, she learns in her wilderness experience a way to live in the world rather than in a carefully selected community of like-minded people. Thus Hagar offers a model of one who surrenders herself to fulfill God's plan, one who uses her desert experience to find hidden strength, one who sees the world in a different way because of her low social status, and finally one who sees herself in an entirely new way and frees herself from the false self that is established by society and culture.

Leah, like Hagar, is used and unloved by those around her. Her sister Rachel is envious of her, because she is fertile while Rachel is barren. Leah contributes a new understanding to spirituality concerning relationships. In spite of her unloving husband, Jacob, she finds that her identity is one that includes him rather than one in opposition to him. In spite of her envious sister, Rachel, Leah responds with compassion and understanding of Rachel's problems. Leah discovers her identity by understanding her role within this complex family structure, rather than by separating herself from Jacob, Rachel, and herself. Leah both gives nurturance and receives it through these relationships.[10]

If we were reared in a seriously dysfunctional family, that could strongly influence our image of God. Linda Hollies illustrates this effectively in the book *Double Stitch* where she describes how her father abused her sexually and physically. What's more, her father would justify his abusive actions with quotations from Sacred Scripture. Her mother tolerated these abuses and seemed to act on the assumption that women become Christ-like by showing no self of their own, by becoming servants of men, and by accepting their abuse. She coped with her painful situation by rationalizations typical of someone reared in a dysfunctional family: don't talk about the issue, don't feel, and be loyal to the family by not talking to outsiders about it. As a young adult, she began attending the United Methodist church with a friend and was attracted to their image of God who was not restrictive. Further she was comforted by their theology that God loved her as she was. This theology comforted her since she was a survivor. At the same time she readily admits she could not trust her father, and still hated him because of the pain he inflicted on her. She concludes her sharing by noting that it took a few years of therapy and a lot of work before she was able to "cut the cords" that bound her to both of her parents and could take her first step toward living life to its fullest.[11]

Our Self-Image

In attempting to know who we are, it's beneficial to reflect on our own personal history. This personal history includes our religious history which means that we grasp something of our early religious training in the first years of our lives, our grade school religious training, and our teenage and adult religious education. Our personal history includes our relationship to our parents and the closeness or the distance we feel toward them. It includes our relationship to our brothers and sisters, our relationship to the children in our neighborhood, and our relationship to our teacher and classmates. Things of this nature help us to understand who we are today, because we have insight into where we are coming from.

Our behavior is indicative of who we are as persons too, because it flows from our being, from our personhood. One individual isolated act doesn't tell us much, but a group of actions do. Patterns of behavior indicate who we are, what our priorities are, and what values we hold highly. If we constantly speak poorly of ourselves, criticizing our physical appearance, our ability to relate to people, and our poor intellectual capabilities, then this pattern indicates we have a poor self-image. At the same time, if we are able to accept compliments from other people and are open to constructive criticism from others, this pattern indicates we have a good self-image.

In examining who we are, some of us are tempted to view ourselves as composed of two separate entities, body and soul. If that is true, is the soul the only really valuable part of our personhood and the body something that is simply tolerated? Do we just view the body as an instrument God made available to us to "save our souls"? Then we probably only tolerate our sexuality and our feelings as well. In reality, body and soul are not separate entities — together they form the whole person which includes sexuality and feelings.[12]

In the initial interview to determine whether applicants are acceptable candidates for a basic quarter of Clinical Pastoral Education, a supervisor may ask them to name five of their strengths and then to indicate five weaknesses. Some have a good knowledge of themselves and a good self-image; as a result they can do this, given sufficient time. Others have little knowledge of themselves and a poor self-image; as a result they can name only a couple of strengths and a couple of weaknesses. They couldn't bring themselves to indicate more weaknesses, because they need to be perfect and cannot accept themselves as imperfect.

All of us need to feel wanted, loved, and accepted, not so much for the work that we do as for being our own unique selves. One of the deepest needs of the human heart is a sense of appreciation and value for who we are. If we are only valued and appreciated for the work we do, then someone else might be able to do the work better and as a result, we would not be valued at all. When we fail to feel appreciated and valued, there is something broken in us. We are not whole.

A student who does not feel accepted by the teacher will not learn as easily. A nurse who doesn't feel accepted by the nursing manager does not find the same job satisfaction. One who does not feel loved and wanted by one's family normally does not recover as quickly after surgery as one who does. A person who lives without experiencing acceptance from significant others is living a life in which a basic human need is not being met.

Acceptance means that the people with whom we live give us a feeling of respect, give us a feeling of being wanted, give us a feeling of being worthwhile. These significant others are happy we are who we are, and they celebrate our uniqueness. Yet, they don't gloss over our idiosyncrasies and shortcomings because that would be living an unreal life. These significant others love us with our limitations. The acceptance we receive from them enables us to be free to grow, free to trust, free to be ourselves. This love and acceptance from others gives us the encouragement to be the unique persons that we are. When we are allowed to display our uniqueness, we become an irreplaceable personality in our household or community. Probably to a lesser extent, the same is true in a work situation; when uniqueness is encouraged and when acceptance of each individual employee is present, then the employees flourish and experience a great degree of job satisfaction.

When we love and accept other people, this does not mean that we deny their defects, that we make excuses for them or explain them away. Neither does it mean that we agree with everything the others do or say. Acceptance means that just the opposite is true; when we deny the limitations of others, we are not accepting the whole person but only one aspect. We certainly have not accepted those persons in the depth of their personhood. Only when we accept the total person with all of their personality traits can we truly say that we accept those individuals.

Negatively, a lack of acceptance means that we don't give other persons the feeling they count or are wanted. We tend to take them for granted or ignore them. We tend to expect nothing from them, and thus indicate our lack of value of them. We who fail to experience acceptance indicate this by our irritating comments and actions, which are clear symptoms of the fact that one of our basic human needs is not being met. Some of these signs are the following three: first, *boasting*: in a subtle or obvious way so that we receive the praise we want so badly; second, *rigidity*: a lack of acceptance causes a lack of security in daily living and the lack of courage to risk one step to either side of the path; third, *inferiority complex*: this simply defines the above conditions. The desire to assert ourselves, to impose ourselves on others, the excessive need for attention, the quick tendency to feel threatened, to exaggerate, or to suspect others of talking about us indicate that we have failed to experience love and acceptance in life.[13]

Just as we manifest signs of others' lack of acceptance of us, so we manifest clear signs of our own acceptance of ourselves. First, we acknowledge our own perceptions, even though they may differ from those of other people. We respect these perceptions, whether they are pleasant or unpleasant. Second, we are aware of our own thoughts and conclusions, our assumptions and judgments. We acknowledge the judgments about ourselves, whether they are affirmative or not. We value our own judgments, whether they agree with others or not. At the same time, we remain open to the possibility of changing our assumptions and judgments as we reevaluate them in the light of new information. Third, we are in touch with our own and others' feelings and value both the painful and the pleasant ones. We permit an awareness of a full range of these feelings, and do not feel a need to sort out unacceptable ones. Fourth, we form immediate and long range goals. We are aware of our intentions and permit an awareness even of unacceptable conditions because they are ours. With difficulty, we are aware of contradictory intentions and struggle to emphasize an appropriate priority. Fifth, we reflect on our actions, realizing that underneath them are thoughts, feelings, and intentions. Finally, we hold certain values which we have freely chosen and correspondingly act on them.[14]

In the past we often spoke of celibacy as unconditional love of God and our neighbor, and we esteemed celibacy because it offered us the opportunity of giving ourselves totally to worship God and to be of service to others in need. Today we might rethink this in the light of insights of modern psychology, and think first of unconditional love of self as a prerequisite for having unconditional love of neighbor and God. If we accept ourselves completely, we are able to love ourselves. This acceptance of self means total acceptance, not just acceptance of the "lovable" aspects of our personality, but our total personhood. In detail, it means that we are called upon to accept our intellectual, spiritual, emotional, and sexual qualities; to accept our femininity, masculinity, heterosexuality, homosexuality, and genitality and to integrate all these into the unique persons that we are.

Jesus once asked his apostles, "Who do people say that I am?" They replied, "Some, John the Baptizer, others, Elijah, still others, one of the prophets." "And you," he went on to ask, "who do you say that I am?" (Mk 8:27-30). Who is Jesus of Nazareth? While it is true that he is "God from God, Light from Light, true God from true God," it is also true that he is at the same time a man like other men, a person who enjoys teaching, a person who spends much time in prayer, a person who is concerned about the poor and the sick and displays his concern through compassion and sensitivity, a person who is hurt, a person who at times becomes angry and frustrated by the lack of faith of other people, a person who enjoyed relaxing with his friends, and finally a person of faith. He had faith in his Father's love for his people and spent his life doing his Father's will, as he mentioned on several occasions in the Gospels. He told us about acceptance and love in his own life by being a person who loved Mary and Martha and Lazarus, who loved Peter, John, James, and Judas too. He taught us by his example and in his words when he commanded us to love God with our whole heart and soul, and to love our neighbor as ourselves. Indirectly, Jesus was telling us that integration is necessary. We need to integrate love, and in order to deeply love anyone, we need to begin at the beginning by loving ourselves as Jesus loved himself, his heavenly Father, and his neighbor.[15]

This integration is not something that is a new insight for us, because it is frequently mentioned in Sacred Scripture. Leviticus (19:18), Matthew (22:37), and 1 John (4:7-21) clearly state that these two go hand in hand. Thomas Aquinas insisted that all knowledge begins with sense knowledge, and he is the most prominent example of the Church's insistence that experience of God needs to be rooted in human experience. Today, theologians are continuing to espouse that idea by insisting that love of neighbor, love of God, and love of self are necessarily intertwined. Karl Rahner clearly supports this idea by stating that love of neighbor and love of God are one. Occasionally, in our Church's history, some, in their desire to be more "spiritual", have downplayed love of neighbor and placed an exaggerated emphasis on love of God, but such an exaggeration needs to be resisted.[16]

When we take a close look at the traditional forms of prayer, this point is illustrated clearly. We used to talk of three levels of prayer, discursive, affective, and contemplative. Discursive prayer was reflective and involved the use of the imagination and the intellect. In discursive prayer we read a passage from Sacred Scripture like the parable of the Prodigal Son and pictured the father hugging his son and welcoming him back. We tried prayerfully to reflect on that scene we imagined in our minds. In this form of prayer, the intellect was used to a large extent. In affective prayer, the emotions were emphasized. Oftentimes, we Roman Catholics use ejaculations to express our affection for God. We pray, "Jesus, I love you; Jesus, I believe in you; Jesus, be with me; Jesus, I trust you; Jesus, forgive me." All of these very brief prayers are affections in the sense that they express our feelings to God. Now if we cannot be emotional in our interpersonal relations with other human beings, how is it possible for us to be emotional or to pray affectively? In other words, how can we say we love God whom we have never seen, if we cannot express love for our friend whom we do see? Thus, there is a clear connection between spirituality and emotionality. Friendship is not only important for our emotional life or for creating intimacy, but it is also important for our spiritual growth.

In forming a close friendship with another person, dependency is created. We are dependent upon the other person to listen to us, to support us, to accept us as we are, to confront us, and to forgive us. These elements are all part of a close friendship with another human being. However, this dependency is not a one way street, but rather each party is dependent upon the other for all these elements. So in friendship there is mutual dependence or an interdependence.

This interdependence is illustrated among five single women in their late thirties and early forties. They are very close friends, frequently dining and going to movies together and vacationing with each other. One of the women commented on how pleasant it was to be able to go to the phone at night and call up a member of the group to alleviate her loneliness, since she lives in an apartment by herself. Another commented that it is nice to have somebody to go out with on a Saturday night instead of just sitting at home. Finally, one woman summed up both statements, "Let's face it, we need one another." This woman indicated that she had insight into friendship — the need of one another for support, for alleviating loneliness, for acceptance, for recreation, etc. Such a person who understands the need of a friend and can admit this dependency, has the capability of readily admitting dependence upon God. If we do not have a close friend upon whom we depend, then how can we experience dependence upon God whom we have never seen? Certainly, it is much more difficult when a close friendship does not exist. Naturally, if we can say, "I need you," to a friend, we can take another step and say, "I love you." Once again, this shows the close connection between affectivity and spirituality.

Forgiveness, Self-Acceptance and Prayer

Today we tend to gloss over many sins and call them something else as we make excuses for them. This reached such heights that several years ago, Karl Menninger wrote a book entitled, *Whatever Became of Sin?* Today William Bennett[17] and others have engaged the debate, but now the talk is about acquiring "virtues" which is the opposite side of the same coin. It is important for us to look at ourselves in our total personhood, and this means to look at our sinfulness as well as our virtuous deeds. All of us are sinners and in accepting ourselves, it is important that we accept that part of us too. When we deny our sinfulness, we are simply fooling ourselves. We are wearing masks in order to cover up our real selves, but as we strive for self-acceptance, it is necessary that we look at every aspect of our personhood. It is beneficial to note that the word "person" which describes our uniqueness is derived from the Latin word "persona" which originally meant "mask." Throughout our lives we play many parts, we assume many roles according to circumstances of time, place, and the other individuals present. As we wear these various masks, we are hiding from ourselves and making it impossible to answer the question, "Who am I?" These masks enable us to run away from ourselves, to forget who we were yesterday, and to fool ourselves into thinking we really are ourselves today. This kind of living makes us disgusted with ourselves because we are so counterfeit and, as a result, we try to lose ourselves in many activities. In this way, we hope to escape our loneliness.

However, prayer can assist in changing this mode of living when it is blended with some human experience of forgiveness and acceptance. With this human experience we are assisted in viewing God as forgiving and accepting, and so are more comfortable in placing ourselves totally in his presence in prayer. As a result, our pretense, hypocrisy, and acting cease as our masks fall off. We see ourselves with our sinfulness, and yet we do not become sad or rush off and commit suicide. We see ourselves as forgiven, accepted, and loved by our kindly heavenly Father, not as condemned or oppressed by him. Through the grace of his acceptance, we are assisted in achieving a better self-acceptance. As a result, our relationships outside of prayer are affected. Now we can more readily receive acceptance and compliments from others, more readily allow our real selves to emerge. Thus our experience of acceptance from God and our friends beneficially affects one another. Ultimately this leads us to realize that we are creatures of a loving Creator, sons and daughters of a tender Father who has created us absolutely unique, utterly original, a human being never to be repeated. With this awareness comes the awareness of the uniqueness of others.[18]

Prayer in the Life of the Pastoral Person

Administering the sacraments, celebrating Masses, visiting the sick, comforting the dying and the bereaved, visiting and caring for sick persons in hospitals, assisting the aged in homes for the elderly, and teaching in parochial schools and C.C.D. programs are just a few of the many ministries open to priests and religious, permanent deacons, lay pastoral ministers, catechists, and many other people who don't hold any special office in the Church, but who are nevertheless the hands and legs of Christ for people who are in need. No matter what ministry a person is involved in, there needs to be a solid foundation for that ministry. That foundation is prayer. Prayer is an indispensable element in a pastoral person's life because without it, nothing in our lives has lasting value. Without it, work in the Lord's vineyard begins to lose its attraction, and becomes boring and a burden. Prayer gives life to our work, zest to our living, meaning to our lives.

Many times it is falsely stated that our work is our prayer, or we haven't time to pray because there is so much work that needs to be done. Other times, we say we pray on the run with momentary acts of formal explicit prayer in the midst of many activities. However, tradition and contemporary experience emphatically indicate that a regular prayer regime is necessary. Without explicit prayer of some length of time, we pastoral persons will not take up our cross and follow Jesus, dying and rising with him. Prayer enables us to distance ourselves from our occupations and allows us to hear the Word of God in a new way, to heal our weaknesses and to restore the power of the Spirit in our lives.[19]

When I think of the necessity of prayer, a workshop on marriage which I attended several years ago comes to mind. The marriage counselor suggested that all married couples spend at least one hour a week together without the children present. During this one hour, the husband and wife were to share with each other the events of the past week and the feelings that accompanied them. Time spent communicating and caring is necessary in order for a marriage to be healthy. If we agree that prayer is a relationship with God, there's only one way to foster growth and to deepen that relationship — time spent alone with Our Beloved. It is also true that it's valuable to share prayer with others, and especially with those with whom we are working.

Prayer is faith and belief in God focused on a personal relationship with him. It is the disclosure of one's self to another in personal dialogue; it is what friends do together. Prayer relates us to the Father, and to Jesus Christ who is our brother as well as Lord, and to the indwelling Spirit who is God living in us. Prayer is a lifelong commitment to know and love God our Creator through Jesus Christ and to share ourselves with him. In prayer, we must be attentive to Christ's presence as we are to our closest friends or spouse. A benefit of our attentiveness to Christ is that we have the opportunity to evaluate our apostolate to see if we are doing God's will or our own, if we are working for God's glory or our own.

If we examine the life of Christ, it is evident that prayer, communication with God, was a frequent element. As he was being baptized by John, he prayed and the Holy Spirit descended upon him while the voice of his heavenly Father said, "This is my beloved Son. My favor rests on him" (Mt 3:17). When Christ took Peter, James, and John up the mountain, he prayed, and while in prayer, he was transfigured before them. In the Garden of Gethsemane with the same three apostles, Jesus knelt in prayer and begged his Father to allow the chalice of suffering and death to pass him by. Before he chose his twelve apostles, he spent forty days in the desert in prayer. The Gospels tell us that Jesus frequently prayed alone, spending the whole night in prayer. On other occasions, he prayed in the presence of his disciples.

The final words of the Book of Revelation, "Come, Lord Jesus" easily serve as the theme of all Christian prayer, because in prayer we attempt to give our undivided attention to the Lord. It is our hope that by conversing and listening, we will deepen our relationship to God through Jesus. This prayer sincerely expressed involves risks, because we are not expressing a desire to learn more facts about God but to encounter him as a person on a deep level of intimacy. A student of history may study the life of Christ to learn all the facts about his life. The same student might learn all about Christ's sermons to discover his ideas and values. A student of literature might study the entire New Testament to learn its literary style. However, when a person of faith cries out from the depths of his being, "Come, Lord Jesus! Come!" he is asking to know God on a personal level. To encounter another person on a deep level is to risk having to change. How many people after they enter a deep relationship with another person in marriage are not changed? Each partner affects the other for better or for worse. Our parents knew this when they warned us in our youth to be careful in selecting our playmates. They knew that friends could affect us, our values, and our behavior. So in our prayer, when we are open to having God become part of our lives, we are risking something of ourselves, risking the possibility of changing and growing.[20]

Prayer can take many forms; it can be words, songs, silence, dance, or the Eucharistic liturgy. It can be done in a group, out in the woods, in the privacy of one's own room, or in the presence of the Blessed Sacrament. However, no matter where it takes place, one thing is sure. Without prayer, the dying and rising of Christ "becomes less operative and cedes to worldly wisdom, the Spirit is muted and one's ministry and personal life tend to be motivated by superficial and selfish considerations."[21]

Conclusion

As pastoral ministers, we need to be spiritual persons who are comfortable with God and comfortable talking about him and sincerely striving to live by his principles. However, it is necessary for us first to be comfortable with ourselves, to feel good about who we are. Once we have accepted ourselves, it is easier for us to acknowledge the Lord's acceptance and love of us. Once we have accepted the forgiveness of others, it is possible for us to accept the Lord's forgiveness. Once we have experienced an in-depth relationship with another human being, it is conceivable that we can form an intimate relationship with God.

However, a good self-image and relationship with other persons are not sufficient; we also need to have a good image of God. Hopefully, we can accept Jesus' invitation to regard God as a loving Father who is readily accessible to us. Then we can enthusiastically share this image with others.

There is an old adage, "You can't give what you don't have." In the area of spirituality, this means that we pastoral persons can't assist others in relating to God unless we ourselves have a relationship with him. It means that only a person who has experienced the Lord's love can speak convincingly about that love.

Footnotes

[1] Barbara Sheahan, "Gender Issues in Supervision," *The Supervision of Pastoral Care*, David A Steere, Ed., Westminster/John Knox Press, Louisville, KY, 1989, pp. 231-232.

[2] Suzanne Beaudoin, "Gospel Figures Show Their Shadows," *Human Development*, Spring, 1988, pp. 6-12.

[3] Audrey E. Campbell-Wray, "Belonging to a Punitive God," *Belonging: Issues of Emotional Living in an Age of Stress for Clergy and Religious*, E.J. Franasiak, Ed., Affirmation Books, Whitinsville, MA, 1979, pp. 54-57.

[4] Peter G. van Breemen, S.J., *As Bread That is Broken*, Dimension Books, Inc., Denville, NJ, 1974, p. 14.

[5] Matthew Fox, *Original Blessing*, Bear & Co. Inc., Santa Fe, NM, 1983, pp. 220-223.

[6] Gerald R. Grosh, S.J., "Theological Presuppositions of Contemporary Ministry," *Spiritual Life*, Fall 1979, pp. 5-8.

[7] Peter G. van Breemen, S.J., *op. cit.*, p. 15.

[8] Timothy E. O'Connell, "Grace and Growth and Growth in Moral Life," The John Neumann Summer Institute, Waterford, WI, July 26, 1979.

[9] Patrick J. McDonald, "Genesis of a Spirituality," *Human Development*, Summer 1993, pp. 33-34.

[10] Carol Ochs, *Women and Spirituality*, Rowman & Allanheld, Totowa, NJ, 1983, pp. 33-44.

[11] Linda H. Hollies, "A Daughter Survives Incest: A Retrospective Analysis," *Double Stitch*, Bell-Scott et. al., Eds., First Harper Perennial, New York, NY, 1993, pp. 152-162.

[12] Nicholas Lohkamp, "Can Education Change Moral Values," The John Neumann Institute, Waterford, WI, August, 1979.

[13] Peter G. van Breemen, S.J., *op. cit.*, pp. 9-11.

[14] Miller, Nunnally and Wachman, *Alive and Aware: Improving Communications in Relationships*, Interpersonal Communications Programs, Minneapolis, MN, 1975, pp. 227-232.

[15] Walter Trobisch, *Love Yourself*, Inter-Varsity Press, Downers Grove, IL, 1982, pp. 9-19.

[16] Philip S. Keane, S.S., "The Meaning and Functioning of Sexuality in the Lives of Celibates and Virgins," *Review For Religious*, March 1975, pp. 280-281.

[17] William J. Bennett, *The Book of Virtues: A Treasury of the World's Great Moral Stories*, Simon and Schuster, New York, NY, 1993.

[18] Donald Goergen, "Affectivity and Spirituality," *Spiritual Counselor*, Tape 4, Thomas More Association, Chicago, IL, 1979.

[19] Eric Doyle, O.F.M., "On Being Human: Reflections on the Anthropological Value of Prayer," *Review For Religious*, November 1974, pp. 1285-1293.

[20] William R. Plat, "Risk Praying," *Emmanuel*, May, 1979, p. 241.

[21] Ernest E. Larkin, O.Carm., and Gerard T. Broccollo, *Spiritual Renewal of American Priesthood*, United States Catholic Conference, Washington, DC, 1973, p. 48.

CHAPTER ELEVEN

THE IMAGE OF GOD
AFFECTS HOW ONE DIES

A S A HOSPITAL CHAPLAIN MINISTERING to the terminally ill, one is constantly exposed to the various emotions the patients experience in their dying process — observing them as they pass through various stages. Tremendous emphasis was given to these stages in Elisabeth Kubler-Ross' book, *On Death and Dying.*

Another interesting dynamic with the terminally ill is to examine the influence the dying person's image of God has on the peace or apprehension with which she/he accepts the dying condition. In speaking of the psychological aspect of religion, Freud viewed God as a projection of the infantile prototype of a human father. He indicated that a father image lay behind every divine figure, and felt that the child vested the unknown and mighty powers of God with the traits of a father figure.[1]

This father image includes both parental figures, the father and the mother. It includes not only the real image of a parent, but also the idealized image of the parent. Some people instead of attributing to God the real characteristics of their parents, attribute characteristics that they wish their parents possessed, or even those which they fear in their parents.

Dr. Earl Loomis, another psychiatrist, adds to Freud's theory the thought that whatever God is in himself and whatever he is to each worshipping community, our concept of God is to a large extent the unwitting work of ourselves. Loomis explains that our image of God reflects our own vision of ourselves. In his theory,

189

there is also room for the idealized self so that our image of God is the person we fantasize we are, rather than the person we are in the minds of many other people. In other words, our ideas and feelings toward God reflect to a great extent our inner expectations and experiences.[2]

A beautiful illustration of projecting our own image onto Almighty God is given by Peter van Breemen in his book, *Certain as the Dawn*. There he notes that a graduate student, while on a directed retreat, imaged God as a huge block of ice with a small light in the center. Later on in that retreat, the young man, who related well with fellow students, realized that he was the huge block of ice and the attractive light in the center was the inner core of himself. He further explained this by noting that even though he was popular with his friends, he felt a distance between himself and them. As a result, he felt like an attractive light which kept people at a distance by his cold outer appearance.[3]

Influences Forming These Images of God

As was indicated earlier, our parents have a strong influence in our formation of an image of God. If our parents communicate themselves as loving and forgiving people, we have a tendency to view God in a similar manner. If they are constantly threatening us with punishment and reminding us of laws to be obeyed, it's natural for us to view God as a lawgiver and a punitive person. On the other hand, if our parents were exceedingly permissive, we tend to view God as finding almost any kind of behavior acceptable.

Our religion teachers and religious leaders too have a significant influence in forming this image of the Almighty. Sometimes religion is presented in a manner in which God is to be feared. Tremendous emphasis is given to God punishing the Jews for their sins of disobedience, and frightening people with his bolts of thunder and flashes of lightning. These same religious leaders may have skipped over the many passages in the Bible which emphasize God as a forgiving, tender person. Quite naturally, we grow up fearing God and viewing him as very distant.

On the other hand, if our religion teachers and leaders presented the word of God as "Good News," God is presented as lovable, compassionate, and caring about us and our welfare. Our attitude toward God is drastically different from the previous group. In this method of teaching, there is significant emphasis on our individual value, lovableness, and worthwhileness. God is viewed, not so much as the Almighty Creator to be feared, but as a loving Father who is approachable and sincerely interested in our everyday problems. God is viewed not so much as transcendent, but as imminent and living in our daily world. In addition to significant religious individuals in our lives, there are secular influences determining our image of God. Certainly teachers, policemen, and other public authority figures in our lives as children helped to mold the image we have of God. So did television and motion pictures.

Our Western culture today does not possess a strong belief in sin. Many find it hard to accept responsibility for their own actions. They tend to blame others, the devil, their genes, their upbringing, their parents for not giving them enough emotional support, etc. So the individual is rarely, if ever, culpable for any breach of God's command. We readily excuse ourselves for our sinful actions. We are told by the television talk-shows that most of our problems will be solved when we build up our self-esteem. Thus as a society we have lost a sense of our need to be saved from sin by Jesus' death and resurrection.

Some Christian churches have even been influenced by this message. As a result, there has been a deemphasis on the reality that we are sinners who are loved by God with all our transgressions and in spite of them. There is evidence of this influence in a couple of popular hymns where a few words have been changed. One of the best known of these is the hymn "Amazing Grace." The original opening stanza goes:

> Amazing grace! how sweet the sound,
> that saved a wretch like me.
> I once was lost, but now am found,
> was blind, but now I see.

In a number of song books the second line has been changed to, "that saved and strengthened me" or "that saved and set me free." John Newton, the author of the hymn, believed that we human beings were "wretches" in desperate need of being saved from sin. These recent adaptations seem to be presenting the idea that we are not sinful people, but are merely suffering from a disability from which we hope to recover. Some imagine God as so understanding of our weakness that he seems to be approving of our immoral behavior.[4]

Psychological, Moral, and Spiritual Development

To understand our image of God thoroughly, it's helpful to investigate our psychological growth and compare that with our growth in spiritual and moral development. In Erikson's eight stages of life, he lists the first as "basic trust vs. mistrust." It is clearly evident that if we have not developed an ability to trust other human beings, it is almost impossible for us to trust God to assist us during a time of need. It is likewise true that if we are stuck in the stage of guilt and cannot move beyond that, it is difficult for us to view God as forgiving. It's equally true that if we have tremendous difficulty establishing intimate relationships with any human person, we will have difficulty establishing an intimate relationship with God. Hence, the link between our psychological and spiritual development is evident.

Lawrence Kohlberg established six stages of moral development which begin in our childhood. He lists the first one as *punishment and obedience* where there is significant emphasis on being obedient to avoid punishment. If we remain in this stage of development, we live life seeking pleasure and avoiding the displeasure of punishment that comes from disobeying. This becomes the norm of goodness for us. His second stage of moral development occurs when a person defines right and wrong on the basis of benefit or reward for that individual. This stage is best described by the phrase, *"reciprocal hedonism."* Both of these first two stages contain a good deal of immaturity. In both, God is viewed as one who rewards and punishes.

The primary motivation for doing good in the third stage is *approval or acceptance* by a respected person in authority. Here there is a shift of emphasis from a physical benefit (candy, money, sex) to an affectional benefit, being regarded as a good boy or good girl. Here, God's approval or blessing is sought. There is a tremendous emphasis on total submission to authority in the fourth stage. The value of law is stressed and there is an orientation toward authority, fixed rules and performing one's duty to preserve order in society. Here God is viewed as a lawgiver, one who gives out rules, "do's and don'ts", and in such a view there is not much room for intimacy.[5]

Thus psychological and moral development are closely related so that as we mature psychologically, we are enabled to grow in our moral development. Our spiritual development is intertwined with this growth too. Ignatian spirituality indicates that the first stage of spirituality stresses whim. This is very similar to the first stage of moral development where the avoidance of punishment and the seeking of pleasure are emphasized. In Ignatius' third stage of development we realize that God loves us, and there is some self-identity attained. At this point, we are working with several issues, namely, an awareness of feelings, a distrust of intimacy and feelings, a low value on relationships, a high value on work and, finally, an emphasis on perfectionism with little emphasis on mercy in our life. The next stage of development for Ignatius is that of being "a loved sinner." When we reach this stage of spirituality, we view God much differently than when we were caught up in the whim stage. Here we are much more capable of viewing God as forgiving and merciful, and of viewing ourselves as acceptable with our sinfulness. Obviously this indicates maturity and psychological growth.

The image of God we have formed influences many aspects of our lives. It affects how we relate to persons in authority as well as those who are responsible to us. It affects how we relate to ourselves, especially when confronted with a crisis like terminal illness. If we view Our Lord as loving us and forgiving our sins, this assists us in accepting our terminal condition. On the other hand, if we image God as distant and punitive, this increases our difficulty in accepting death and possibly causes us to interpret sickness and death as punishment. As a result, we fear judgment from God at our death. On the other hand, if we imagine God to be very permissive so that he doesn't expect much of us, this prompts us to lose our consciousness of sin, not be aware of our need for forgiveness, and not to be fearful of God or his judgment.

Procedures and Methods Used

In each of the two surveys I conducted, nine terminally ill persons were interviewed. The purpose was to determine the influence the dying person's image of God has on the peace or apprehension with which she/he faces death. In the 1981/1982 survey, three women and six men were interviewed and their ages ranged from 36 to 72. Two of the participants were in their 30's, three were in their 50's, one in her 60's, and three in their 70's. Five of them were married, two were single, one was divorced, and one was widowed. Even though all of them at one time in their lives had received some Christian education, it seems that four out of the nine persons were very religious (frequently attended church before their sickness, often prayed at home, and lived Christ's values to a great extent), two were slightly religious (rarely participated in church and rarely prayed) and three were someplace in the middle.

In the 1993/1994 survey, three women and six men were interviewed and their ages ranged from 51 to 83. Four of the participants were in their 50's, three in their 70's, and two in their 80's. Seven of the participants were married, one was single, and one was widowed. Eight out of the nine members received a religious education as children, but four of them had given up the practice of their religion, and one who received no religious education never did practice any religion. This means four of them frequently attended their church before their sickness, often prayed at home, and attempted to live out the values of Jesus Christ.

The empirical method of research was used in preference to

the bibliographical method, so the surveys are based on observation and experience rather than on listing the current writings in the literature related to this subject of how a person's image of God influences their impending death. In these surveys, several steps were followed in interviewing the dying patient. First, only that patient was selected who had a terminal illness and the person's sex, age, intellectual competency, religious activity, or race made no difference. In fact, an effort was made to interview terminally ill persons as vastly different from one another as possible.

Second, only those patients were selected who had a clear knowledge of their terminal condition. Generally, these patients were in the final stages of their illness, but they had six months or more to prepare for death. Third, the surveys were conducted as effective chaplaincy took place, and during this ministry special emphasis was noted of the patient's concept of God as well as of his/ her comfortableness or uncomfortableness with the terminal condition. Fourth, additional information concerning the patient was gleaned from relatives and nursing personnel so that a more complete picture of the patient could be obtained.

Results of the 1981/1982 Survey

Three of the nine patients seemed to be at peace with God and to accept their dying condition calmly. No real names are used to protect the patients' privacy. Peter viewed God as very forgiving, and this enabled him to experience God as forgiving him the sins of his life and thus making him acceptable to his Creator. John experienced God as a Good Shepherd who cared for him vicariously through the Blessed Virgin Mary, who was a good provider and protector during crisis. Martha viewed salvation as something that a person earned, and seemed to view herself as having attained that. For her it was similar to having studied daily throughout a semester of school and having successfully passed the exam. She was confident she had passed the course and won the prize of eternal life.

Four other patients seemed fearful or very fearful of death, and two of the four had less than one month to face their condition when I met them. Sarah viewed God as distant and punitive and even though she had led a good life, she was still uncomfortable with the thought of meeting God, the Great Judge and the All-Powerful Creator. George, who had led a good life and was very active in his church, regarded God as a rewarder and punisher, and judged that he did not measure up to God's high standards. Mike felt his life was fairly sinful, and regarded God as punitive and aloof. He struggled to accept the Lord's forgiveness as he faced death with great fear. Dan, the final person in this group, experienced God as very hostile, as one who had only given him pain. Since God never gave him much happiness or love in this life from his perspective, he could not accept that God would give him anything good when it came to dying.

The other two persons in the survey, Jim and Ruth, seemed to vacillate between peace and anxiety in the final days. Even though Jim prayed frequently, he viewed God as demanding perfection of his creatures and naturally this stirred up fear. At other times he seemed to believe in a merciful God who forgave his sins. This brought peace to him. Ruth perceived God to be strict, but good. Again the concept of "measuring up" was present. So peace or apprehension existed depending upon which aspect of God was being emphasized at the moment.

In conclusion, this survey indicates that their image of God had a clear relationship with their ability to cope with the dying process. A person's prayerfulness and living Christian values did not guarantee that they faced death with tranquility. In fact, some people who were very religious did not experience this. The peaceful death seemed to occur because the person had a spiritual conviction that God was loving and forgiving and calling the person home. Another factor is time to accept death. It seemed that those who died with only a little time to prepare do not do as well as those who had six months or more to accept it. However, there is a possibility for a person to face death with no feeling or meaning because that's the way she/he existed in life.

Results of the 1993/1994 Survey

I conducted a similar survey with nine dying patients 12 years later with the help of Lathe Snyder, a chaplain at a hospice in Cincinnati, Ohio. Again, no real names are used here.

Adam was unsure whether God existed or not. He enjoyed philosophizing about the world and religions, but was not convinced there was a higher ultimate power. However, he believed that if there was a God, he would be kind and understanding; he would be like a father who wants all his children to be spared any kind of pain and to share with them forever all the wonderful blessings he possessed. As a result, he seemed to be at peace when death came.

In spite of Mark's Christian upbringing, he stopped practicing his religion in his late teens. At the same time he viewed God as very permissive, understanding, and forgiving. As a result, he thought God did not become angry with people who failed to acknowledge him in prayer, but understood their human frailties. He seemed to be at peace as death approached. Mike was very similar to Mark. He did not practice any religion and did not pray at home. His image of God was the same. It seems to me that both of them had an image of God similar to the movie, *Oh, God!* where George Burns played God and John Denver, his prophet to the people. God was humorous, kind, friendly, and never got angry even though John Denver was very slow to understand his unique call. God was a *laissez faire* deity for these men.

The next patient, John, was very religious and viewed God as a caring and providential father as Jesus described his Father in one of his sermons, "Look at the birds in the sky; they neither sow nor reap, nor gather into barns, and yet your heavenly Father feeds them. Are you not of much more value than they?" (Mt 6:26). So John believed that God would kindly care for him since God is concerned about his creations of lesser value. Joyce was very similar to John in her religious practices as well as in her concept of God.

Gertrude was a very religious individual. In her prayer life she spoke of God as a friend, Savior, and a kindly Father. Hence, when death came, she had a peaceful countenance.

Ron did not practice any religion and was not a prayerful individual. At the same time he was difficult to understand, because he viewed God as very demanding and rigid but at the same time loving and accepting. Even though I could not understand a person conceiving such an image of God, he spoke of death calmly. Thus, I guess he met the expectations of this demanding loving God.

Sam, on the other hand, was fearful of dying. He did not practice any religion, and viewed God as distant and punitive. As a consequence, he approached death with fear and dread. Pam was similar to a few of the people in the first survey. She was very religious, praying daily and reading the Scriptures frequently. In addition, she seemed to live out her beliefs in her daily life. Yet when death became evident, she was fearful and faced it with anxiety.

A More Detailed Account of Four Patients from the 1993/1994 Survey

Mike was a 57-year-old married man who suffered from inoperable cancer of the throat. As a boy he had been "saved" as a result of attending Sunday school and church, but he hadn't been active in the practice of his religion for over 30 years. When asked about his image of God, he said that God was the Creator of everything. He made the heavens, and that is where Mike hoped to go. Heaven for him was a place of joy where you lived happily and peacefully with all of your loved ones. Mike admitted that he sinned like everyone else, but that God is merciful and forgiving. Mike regretted that he stopped going to church, but excused himself to some extent by saying that he worked seven days a week for many years, and just got out of the habit of attending church services. He also regretted that he didn't spend more time with his children, failing to do some things with them that he should have. Because of his belief in the mercy of God and to some extent his excusing himself for some of his failures, he faced God with confidence.

Joyce was a 57-year-old married woman who was very religious in her life. As she realized death was approaching quickly, she wanted to receive the "last rites" of her church so that she could have her passport to heaven. She viewed heaven as an island, because she was happiest as a child living near the water where she enjoyed fishing frequently. She was comfortable with God and dying because, "God is my friend. I feel that I can lean against his shoulder and he will support me. He has helped me in the past and he will help me in the future." She went on to say that she can't pray her regular prayers anymore because she gets so distracted. So, now in the last two weeks of her life she mentioned that she just talks to God like a friend, telling him what's on her mind. She feels God is listening to her because he is her friend. Naturally she was comfortable with the idea of meeting such a God in death.

Mark was a 71-year-old married man who was active as a youth in his religion, but presently hadn't prayed much or practiced his religion for years. He admitted that he had done some things that have been wrong, but balanced that with the fact that we have all of us done some wrong. As he approached death, he said he was anxious not about dying, but about the unknown in the process in dying. What comes after death? How painful will dying be? Specifically, he said he did not fear any punishment from God.

Pam was a 52-year-old married woman who was very religious. She had gone to church most of her life and had prayed at home with some frequency. She suffered from terminal cancer and approached death with tremendous fear and apprehension. She had told a number of people, including two clergymen, that she was fearful of going to hell. Both of these clergy persons tried to ease her pain by reaching the source of her fear, but were unable to do so. Her pastor assured her that all she had to do was to repent of whatever it was she had done wrong and God would forgive her. Yet she held on to her guilt feelings, responding, "Some things can never be forgiven." It seemed she was terrified of death.

Conclusion

As you can readily see, the results of the recent survey were very different from the earlier one. Seven out of the nine people seemed to approach death in a relaxed manner, while only two viewed death with fear. This contrasts with the previous survey where only three people faced death calmly. All of those who approached death with a peaceful attitude did not have the same image of God; however, the two who feared death had a similar characteristic of viewing God as punitive and very demanding.

The reasons for the difference in the results of the two surveys seem to be several. First, a number of people today seem to be in the second stage of moral development, where convenience and personal pleasure strongly influence moral judgments. This is associated with our permissive society, where all ideas are supposedly of equal value and all kinds of behavior need to be accepted or else one is narrow-minded.

Thirty years ago it seems that many people were in the fourth stage. Obedience to God and country ruled the day. Even twenty years ago in the Watergate era, some of those found guilty of breaking the law excused themselves on the basis that they simply were being obedient to their superior. However, as they were given their sentences for their criminal acts, the judge told them that blind obedience is not a virtue. This influences our relationship with God and our image of God.

Another reason seems to be that today we readily excuse ourselves and fail to take responsibility for our actions. This was best expressed in a cartoon where a man is sitting in his living room watching the evening news in disbelief as the commentator says, "The trial was abruptly halted when the defendant agreed to plead guilty to all charges but denied any wrongdoing."

Related to this attitude is that people seem to have lost a sense of sin and a feeling of fear. People don't fear contracting disease by having sex with multiple partners, don't fear punishment for engaging in acts of violence, and don't fear going to hell. What they seem to fear is that their image might be tarnished if they are caught or implicated somehow in a crime.

A final reason for the difference seems to be that we Americans are strong believers in our independence and privacy in forming our own conscience. Instead of seeking wisdom from others more knowledgeable than ourselves, the teachings of the Church, or a spiritual counselor, we prefer to form our consciences in isolation today or go along with the majority concerning the morality of certain types of behavior.

Dr. Richard Meyer, an oncologist in Cincinnati, Ohio, said that his patients are not so fearful of dying today as they were previously, because people are kept alive so long that they are willing to die as an escape from the painful process of living. His experience is that the patients fear pain and the dehumanizing process of dying, and that they fear pain more than the judgment of God. This is especially true in his practice of very old people, and terminally ill cancer patients. His second reason for believing that people are not so fearful of death today is that people have lost a consciousness of sin which was an idea that was expressed earlier.

Even though I did not encounter such a person in this survey, provision needs to be made for an indifferent person as Meursault in Albert Camus' book, *The Stranger*. Although he was on death row, Meursault was indifferent toward his approaching execution. When a priest attempted to minister to him assuming he had fears about his imminent death, Meursault physically evicted him from his cell. However, Meursault had long been an enigma to others because of his indifference toward life. His feelings were so repressed that the only spirited activity which he engaged in was an occasional and unpredictable act of violence. Since he was so estranged from his own person, life's ending was as meaningless as life itself.

In sharing the results of my surveys with others in the helping professions, my hope is they will influence their interactions with the dying. Hopefully those ministering to the dying will be more aware that a person's image of God is one factor influencing his/her dying condition. We who minister to the dying might challenge appropriately those patients whose image of God is different than that presented by Jesus. We can't expect significant changes in peoples' attitudes, but small changes that will make their dying a little more comfortable, that will enable their image of God the Father to be more like that of the God of Abraham, Isaac, Jacob, and Jesus.

Survey in 1981/1982

Patient's Name*	Age	Marital Status	Religiousness**	Image of God	Attitude Toward Death
Sarah	69	widow	fairly religious	distant & punitive	fearful & anxious
George	56	married	very religious	rewarding & punishing	very fearful
Mike	36	divorced	poor religious	punitive & aloof	very fearful
Dan	55	married	poor religious	hostile	very fearful
Jim	72	single	very religious	perfectionist	wavers between peace and fear
Ruth	72	married	fairly religious	strict but fair judge	wavers between peace and fear
Peter	39	married	fairly religious	forgiving	peaceful
John	78	married	very religious	Good Shepherd	peaceful
Martha	56	single	very religious	loving but demanding judge	peaceful

* No real names are used in this paper and some circumstances have been altered to protect the patient's privacy.

** Determined by a person's attendance at church, prayer life, and living the values of Christ.

Survey in 1993/1994

Patient's Name*	Age	Marital Status	Religiousness**	Image of God	Attitude Toward Death
Adam	80	married	none	if God exists, he is not mean	peaceful
Sam	75	married	non-practicing	distant & punitive	peaceful
Gertrude	75	widowed	very religious	friend, Savior, Father	peaceful
Mark	71	married	non-practicing	permissive, understanding & forgiving	peaceful
John	83	single	very religious	caring & providential Father	peaceful
Joyce	57	married	religious	loving & caring	peaceful
Mike	57	married	non-practicing	understanding, permissive & forgiving	peaceful
Pam	52	married	very religious	punitive & just	fearful
Ron	59	married	non-practicing	demanding & rigid, but loving	peaceful

* No real names are used in this paper and some circumstances have been altered to protect the patient's privacy.

** Determined by a person's attendance at church, prayer life, and living the values of Christ.

Footnotes

[1] Sigmund Freud, *The Future of an Illusion*, Hogarth Press, London, England, 1928, p. 33-34.

[2] Earl A. Loomis, Jr., *The Self in Pilgrimage*, Harper & Row, New York, NY, 1960, pp. 13-15.

[3] Peter G. van Breemen, S.J., *Certain As the Dawn*, Dimension Books, Denville, NJ, 1980, p. 11.

[4] Brian Abel Ragen, "A Wretch Like Who?", *America*, America Press Inc., New York, NY, 1994, pp. 8-11.

[5] David G. Benner, ed., *Baker Encyclopedia of Psychology*, Baker Book House, Grand Rapids, MI, 1985, pp. 722-724.

CHAPTER TWELVE

ALL THE EMPLOYEES ENGAGING IN MINISTRY

B ERNIE, A RESIDENT OF A SMALL TOWN in Kentucky, went deer hunting at 5:00 a.m. on a Saturday in December. Failing to spot any deer, he returned to his cabin at 11:00 a.m. where he and his wife had lunch. Their cabin was located near a wooded area and even though his wife never hunted with him, she would accompany him from home some 60 miles away so he would have some companionship at their cabin.

After lunch she returned to her quiet reading, while he returned to his deer hunting. Bernie never hunted deer on the ground. He preferred his "deer-stand." This apparatus is about 25 feet high in a tree, and its purpose is to give the hunter something solid to stand on as he searches for the deer for some distance in several directions.

About 4 o'clock that Saturday afternoon, the weather turned ominous. The clouds darkened and the wind began to blow fiercely. Its force increased quickly, blowing his rifle against the tree frequently. Before he had a chance to climb down the tree, a big gust of wind blew him out of his "deer-stand" onto the ground. He fell about 25 feet landing on his right hip, causing the socket to fracture and the upper part of his leg to go into his pelvic area. He also suffered a hemorrhage in the fall. He lay on the ground in shock for a few minutes and then he tried to get up, but immediately fell to the ground. At this point he realized that his leg and hip were broken.

He had a four-wheel all-terrain vehicle, but that was about two miles away from him. He grabbed his gun and began to crawl, realizing that he would freeze to death in this 24 degree temperature if he did not get back to his wife and cabin before long. Even though he was wearing his hunting suit which helped to keep him warm, he began to feel the cold of the ground. At this point he knew his only chance to survive was to attempt to crawl back to his all-terrain vehicle.

Intense pain overtook him as he began moving toward his vehicle. However, he realized that there was only one other choice left for him and that was to die in the woods. So in spite of the pain, he used all of his energy to continue crawling back. Finally after two hours of intense pain and crawling, he reached his vehicle. Initially he tried to pull himself up in the vehicle but could not do so. Then he mustered all of his energy and grabbed the steering wheel to pull himself up. He started the vehicle and began driving toward his cabin as darkness began to settle in. It was almost 7 o'clock when he came into an open area out of the woods, and saw his wife who was looking for him. She knew something was wrong since he did not return at 5 o'clock for their supper.

When they got back to the cabin, he had to be transferred from this vehicle to his pickup truck. The wife could not do this by herself, so she ran to another cabin that was a couple of hundred yards away and enlisted the assistance of an 18-year-old young man. This teenager came to help Bernie get into the truck, but each time the neighbor and Bernie's wife tried to move him the pain was excruciating. When he screamed from the top of his lungs because of the intensity of the pain, his wife and the neighbor stopped their efforts to move him. At the same time the wounded hunter realized that he had to be taken to the hospital in order to save his life, so he instructed them, "Move me to the pickup truck no matter how loud I scream." Eventually they made it.

Another problem they encountered was that the wife could

not drive at night since she had sight only in one eye and the 18-year-old did not have any driver's license or experience in driving. Yet he was the only one who could see, so Bernie instructed him how to start the truck and how to slowly drive it to the hospital. Even though the lad had never driven a truck before, he was able to negotiate all the bends in the road and finally got to a small hospital. The hospital personnel were totally amazed that Bernie survived this long from his severe accident. At this point he was suffering from hypothermia in addition to his other problems. They took off his hunting suit and clothed him with warm towels in order to elevate his temperature. At the same time, the doctor and the nurses there realized that they could not treat him because of the severity of his injuries. They transported him by ambulance to a larger hospital where complete recovery occurred six weeks later.

This story illustrates not only the events in a brave man's life, but what can be done when a person has a strong reason to attain a goal. As he told me, "I didn't want to die alone and I wanted to get back to my wife." Bernie had a will to live, so he never gave up crawling even though he was "frozen" and suffered intense pain. This brings to mind the admonition of Victor Frankl, "If there is a will there will be a way," that is, if we discover a reason for accomplishing something, then we will find the means to attain that goal.

If we reflect on God's creation and his invitation that we care for his gift of creation, possibly that will give us a reason for forming a work ethic based on God. If we reflect on our baptismal commitment and on the documents of Vatican II which indicate that all people have received a vocation, a calling by God to share in creating a better world, maybe that will give us a reason to believe that all of us are called to minister.

Forming a Work Ethic Based on God

Medieval Christians understood the world to be a gift and a task from God. This gift needed to be molded and shaped like clay in the hands of a potter. It was not to be placed in a corner of the room and forgotten. To accomplish this, these medieval Christians formed crafts and guilds (labor organizations). Thus, these workers cultivated a Christian work ethic, that is, an attitude of incorporating their beliefs in the work place.

This work ethic provides Christians and all God-fearing people with a spiritual view of work which enables them to give new meaning to their undertakings. They have a different attitude about work. It is no longer simply a task to be performed or a means of "putting bread on the table and clothes on our backs," but a means of cooperating with God in creating a better world. The basis for this belief about work is that God has called everyone to some productive vocation, which is the means of serving the common good and giving greater glory and honor to God. To some extent this is based on Victor Frankl's theory of a "search for meaning" and Ignatius of Loyola's motto of "all for the honor and glory of God."

Work does not just mean that activity performed between 8:30 a.m. and 5:00 p.m. It also includes reading, homemaking, leadership in the civic community, planting flowers, helping shut-ins and caring for children. It makes no difference whether pay is involved or not. All of us are expected to do our part in making the world a better place to live. We are all called to be co-creators with God.

Ed Marciniak, president of the Institute of Urban Life at Loyola University in Chicago, gives three examples to illustrate this concept. He speaks initially of the first woman to sit in a president's cabinet, Frances Perkins. She was the U.S. Secretary of Labor under Franklin Delano Roosevelt from 1933 to 1945. She once said, "I came to Washington to work for God, FDR, and millions of forgotten, plain, common working men." Frances Perkins had a definite notion of blending her work with her religious convictions.

A second example is that of a man, not a Catholic, who reads two publications regularly. One is the *Wall Street Journal* and the other is *The Catholic Worker Magazine*. He wants to become the best worker he can at his job, and at the same time bring God into his work place. He has little use for the kind of religion whose God cannot somehow be found in his daily work.

A third example taken from an article in the *National Catholic Worker* which denigrated the young men and women who had devoted a year or two of their lives as Jesuit Volunteers. It criticized these people because the majority of former Jesuit Volunteers entered well-paying careers as lawyers, accountants, and statisticians. Fortunately, a Jesuit Volunteer from Boston corrected this notion, saying that these people were now expressing their service to others in ways other than working full time in a soup kitchen.[1]

God encounters men and women individually seeking a personal response. He gives them the world as a gift and a task. Thus the development of a God-based work ethic is the responsibility of each person. We cannot expect someone else to do it for us, someone else to hand us a prepackaged work ethic, because it is formed from *"a set of values which gives meaning to our daily work, establishes priorities, orders hope and desires, justifies deferred expectations and helps us cope with the world's sins and suffering."*[2]

"More than mere work, business is a vocation," said Joe Sciortino at a conference in Miami. The chairman of Sysco Food Service, who helped organize the conference on business as a vocation sponsored by the Miami Archdiocesan Office of Lay Ministry, went on to say, "Business is a Christian vocation in which people take dominion over creation and act in a productive manner as Scripture demands."

Archbishop Edward A. McCarthy set the background for the ideas expressed by Mr. Sciortino as he opened the conference, saying that we need to regain the concept of business as a valued service to the human community and to make a connection between our faith and our business.

At this same conference Emilie Griffin urged the audience to discover the Lord not only in the beautiful hillside, but in the office corridors, the factory, and the board room. Fr. John Haughey, S.J. built on that theme by suggesting that people are leading split lives, separating Sunday from their work week. He admonished the people to have a connection between their faith and their daily activities. Specifically, he urged them to search where the Heavenly Father was working in their lives and then to ask for the "grace of God at work in the work."[3]

Donald R. Patterson suggested specific means of attaining the goals expressed at this conference in his article in *Liguorian Magazine*. There he emphasized the value of people dedicating their work to God by beginning each day with a brief prayer asking God to bless their endeavors as they commit them to him. Secondly, he urged that people change their attitude about work by recognizing its true value. Too often he thought people look upon their jobs as unimportant and valueless, instead of finding merit in them. He added that the trash collector who keeps the streets clean provides a service equal to the administrator who manages that community. The spouse who cleans, cooks, and does the shopping plays as important a role in the life of a family as the one who earns the salary. All these people are doing tasks that absolutely need to be performed for the well-being of society and the family.[4]

All People Receive a Call to Minister

In many hospitals sponsored by religious groups, there are various programs for new and veteran employees to instill in them the values of the institutions. New employees usually begin on Monday morning at 8 a.m. when an orientation program is presented to them. Some of them begin with a slide/video presentation outlining the history of the persons who founded the hospital. Then, there is another video giving the new personnel a history of the institution, with an emphasis on the compassion and self-giving of the founders of the hospital and some of its heroes, both religious and lay people.

A pastoral care person often follows with a presentation which includes an explanation of the philosophy and mission of the hospital. She/he concludes with a challenge for all the employees in every department to carry on the institution's mission, and in a real sense to be ministers of God's word in action.

Most new employees can't believe what they just heard. They

were hired to be nurses, X-ray technicians, and environmental workers, not ministers. They hadn't gone to any Bible school, and besides many viewed themselves as unworthy to be ministers of God. That was for other people who were "good" and called specially by God for a unique task. For these people, the salvation of the world is the task only of the full-time minister.

However, Vatican II made it very clear that this is the function of the whole Church. This Council defined that the Church is the people of God, not just the clergy and religious. So everyone is expected to evangelize the world by sharing Jesus' values. For Christians this obligation flows from our baptismal vows because we are expected to bring the "good news" of God to others.

Pope John Paul II expressed a similar idea in his first encyclical, where he spoke of all the followers of Christ as disciples. He stated that the Church is a community of disciples and the people of God, saying:

"Therefore if we wish to keep in mind this community of the people of God which is so vast and so extremely differentiated, we must see first and foremost Christ saying in a way to each member in the community, 'Follow Me.' It is the community of the disciples, each of whom in a different way — at times very consciously and consistently but other times not very consciously and very consistently — is following Christ."[5]

This reference to the Church as a community of disciples is applicable, not only to all members of the Catholic Church but to every Christian, since all of us through our baptisms have heard that call of Christ to come and follow him. This concept of the followers of Jesus as disciples has a biblical basis, especially in the Acts of the Apostles. In Acts 6:1, St. Luke says "as the number of disciples grew" and in verse 2 "the twelve assembled the community of disciples," meaning all the followers of Christ.[6]

It is important that the people understand that the call to follow Christ is not coming from some Church official but from the Lord Jesus himself. In this way Jesus becomes the focal point of the Christian life. A disciple is by his/her very definition, one who has not yet arrived but rather is a learner who is in the process of comprehending the values and the message of Jesus Christ. To be a disciple is like being a student trying to understand the master's teachings and ways. To be a disciple means that one is on the way to follow the master more completely and perfectly. This is what all of us are about in any church. The Acts of the Apostles described the early Church as one in which the disciples of Christ were on an adventure following him in new and ever-changing situations. The disciples of Christ today are on a similar pilgrimage and are expected, as the first disciples were, to share the Good News and to build the Kingdom of God.[7]

All engaged in hospital ministry or any work have the opportunity with their imperfect faith and less than perfect lives to imitate the people in the Bible as they work in the Lord's vineyard. They can bring God's love to the patients and to one another as they live their daily lives. They can do this by implementing some Christian standards of service that most health facilities and businesses expect of their employees:

1. Treat all persons with compassion, care, courtesy, and respect.
2. Respond quickly.
3. Take time to be helpful.
4. Respect the privacy/dignity of others.
5. Always give clear, concise explanations.
6. Practice good listening skills.
7. Maintain an appropriate environment.
8. Look the part.
9. Deal with a difficult situation effectively.
10. Perform as a member of a team.[8]

The hope in expressing these ideas is to challenge all of us engaged professionally in pastoral care to remember our unique calling to minister, and to stir up within ourselves those initial feelings of fervor to be of service to others. Certainly if God expects all his people to exemplify in their daily living Christ's values, much more so does Our Lord expect this of pastoral care people. So hopefully these thoughts will stir into flame our original zeal for the glory of the Lord. Secondly, it is hoped that these ideas will broaden our concept of ministry. It is not just to the patients, their families, and the staff who have personal problems. It is so that the pastoral staff facilitates all employees to join us in sharing the Good News of Jesus Christ with others. Collaborating with others in ministering in the name of Jesus Christ and living out his values are essential in the Making of a Pastoral Person.

Footnotes

1 Ed Marciniak, "Toward a Catholic Work Ethic," *Origins*, February 25, 1988, Washington, DC, pp. 631 & 633.

2 Ed Marciniak, *op. cit.*, p. 632.

3 Araceli M. Cantero, "Business is Our Christian Vocation," *Catholic Telegraph Register*, Cincinnati, OH, September 14, 1990, p. 3b.

4 Donald Ray Patterson, "Labor Day — Eight Ways to Bless Our Daily Work," *Liguorian Magazine*, Liguori, MO, September, 1990, pp. 65-66.

5 John Paul II, *Redemptor Hominis*, March 4, 1979, U.S. Catholic Conference, Washington, DC, 1979, #21, pp. 89-90.

6 Avery Dulles, *A Church to Believe In*, Crossroad Publishing Co., New York, NY, 1984, pp. 7-9.

7 Avery Dulles, *op. cit.*, pp. 9-11.

8 "Standards of the Service First Program" at the Good Samaritan Hospital, Cincinnati, OH, 1991.

CHAPTER THIRTEEN

IMPERFECT PEOPLE DO EFFECTIVE MINISTRY

Some students feel overwhelmed after reading about all the characteristics and skills needed to be effective in giving people pastoral care. Some feel guilty when they realize that they haven't ministered in the most effective manner. Others initially are depressed by all the demands on a pastoral care person. These feelings are understandable, but it's helpful to remember that even though we don't do things perfectly, our ministry can still be effective and lead people to God. It's important to search in the Scriptures for imperfect persons whom God chose to accomplish great tasks.

The Samaritan Woman

As we read the Gospels, we readily see that the people Jesus chose for special tasks were imperfect. In John's fourth chapter, we have the account of the Samaritan woman at the well. This woman had been married five times; she was a social outcast in her community, and that is the reason she came to the well around noon. Most other women came in the early morning or in the late evening when the sun was not at its height. But she came at noon since she was a marginal member of her community.

Jesus, being thirsty after a long dusty walk, invited her to be his follower by initially requesting a drink from her. He invited her to believe in him by stating that people who drank of the water that he would give, would never thirst again because he would provide a fountain within people to give eternal life. The woman accepted his invitation and requested to have this water so that she would never thirst again. This was the beginning of her faith.

Once she believed, Jesus challenged her by asking her to bring her husband. Embarrassingly she responded that she had no husband, and Jesus immediately replied, "You are correct because your present husband is not your real husband since you have had five already." Jesus concluded this interaction by inviting her to believe that he is the Messiah, the Anointed One of God.

Immediately the woman went to the village and announced to the people who Jesus was, saying, "He told me everything I ever did." Next she invited the Samaritans to come out to see Jesus and to hear him themselves. At this point we see the Lord's work taking place because she gave witness to Jesus; she urged people to follow him and accept his teachings and values. Here she was truly a disciple, but an imperfect follower. She did not fully believe. Her faith was not mature but still she did the Lord's work. This section concludes with the Samaritans saying to her, "No longer does our faith depend upon your story, we have heard for ourselves and we know that this really is the saviour of the world." Finally, it's significant that she believed in Jesus on two issues, namely, as a source of life-giving water and as the Messiah.

The Man Born Blind

In the ninth chapter of John's Gospel, we have another occurrence of ministry by a person who has imperfect faith. This is the man born blind. Jesus began the section by announcing "I am the light of the world." Then he cured the man of his blindness. The Pharisees became upset by this healing because it occurred on the Sabbath, so they found the blind man who told them that Jesus was the one who cured him. At this point the blind man invited the Pharisees to believe. Once he informed them how the cure took place, they rejected this: "Jesus could not be from God since he performed the healing on a Sabbath." However, others objected stating that if Jesus were a sinner he could not perform healings like this. So the Pharisees were sharply divided. This section of the Bible concludes as the former blind man testified regarding Jesus, "He is a prophet."

The Pharisees still weren't satisfied, so they asked the former blind man to tell them again how he was able to see. The man asked them whether they wanted to become Jesus' disciples, to which they retorted scornfully, "You are the one who is that man's disciple." Here the Pharisees identified the healed man as a "disciple of Jesus." Shortly after this the man of newly formed faith testified again about Jesus to the Pharisees: "It is unheard of that anyone ever gave sight to a person blind from birth. If this man were not from God, he could never have done such a thing." Even though this man was a very recent believer in Jesus, he testified twice about the Lord's identity to the Pharisees and other bystanders who overheard the conversation. He led some people to Christ with his immature faith.

The Apostle Peter

The apostle Simon Peter is another example of a person who led people to God. When Christ asked the apostles to identify who he was in Matthew's 16th chapter, Simon spoke up in front of the others saying, "You are the Messiah, the Son of the living God." Jesus commented favorably about Simon's faith, giving him the nickname "Rock, Peter." Later, when Jesus predicted that he was going to suffer and die, Peter objected. Then Jesus called him by another name, saying, "Get behind me Satan."

In Luke's passion narrative Jesus addresses Peter:

"Simon, Simon! Remember that Satan has asked for you,

to sift you all like wheat. But I have prayed for you that your faith may never fail. You in turn must strengthen your brothers." "Lord," he said to him, "at your side I am prepared to face imprisonment and death itself." Jesus replied, "I tell you, Peter, the rooster will not crow today until you have three times denied that you know me" (Lk 22:31-34).

After Peter's denial, he was among the apostles who deserted Christ as he was executed on the cross. Christ chose this impetuous, sometimes weak man to engage in significant ministry, to be the leader of his Church.

The Apostle Paul

In one letter, Paul struggled to put into words a theme that flowed from the core of his being, that is, what "being in Christ" meant to him. In his words he says, "For to me life means Christ and dying is so much gain" (Ph 1:21). A paraphrase of this thought that gets close to the sense of the verse is that for Paul living simply means Christ so that if Paul died, he merely gains more of Christ because in heaven he will see him face to face, and not hazily as through a mirror. Paul's tremendous love for Christ and desire for union with him is expressed in Galatians too:

> "I have been crucified with Christ. The life I now live is not my own but the life where Christ lives in me; and my present bodily life is lived by faith in the Son of God who loved me and gave himself up for me" (Gal 2:20).

It's important to realize that this concept was so intimate and deeply personal with Paul that he could not express the idea without sometimes using the singular personal pronouns, "who loved me and gave himself up for me."

Another response to his deep desire for union with Christ

causes Paul to become a great missionary who wants all Gentiles to be united with Christ too. He goes on three missionary journeys and writes a number of letters to his converts to attain this goal. He also endures shipwrecks, beatings, and imprisonment for this goal. Another reason he expended so much energy was that he was a passionate pastor. He wants the best for himself and his converts, and naturally he becomes very upset when anyone distorts the truth he imparted to them.

When opponents called in question Paul's message or his apostleship, he sometimes defends himself with a historical account in which he asserts that God is the one who called him to be an apostle. At other times Paul defends himself by attacking his opponents as if he were assaulting an enemy's camp. C.H. Dodd agrees with this impression, stating that Paul had a hot and quick temper which is readily evident in Galatians and 2 Corinthians.[1] It seems that it would have been more helpful for Paul to be more open and direct with his anger instead of resorting to hostile criticisms, assailing the sincerity of others and attacking their character, especially when he fails to provide a reasoned criticism of his opponent's viewpoint. He not only attacks his opponents directly but also indirectly as he lists the many things he has suffered in the service of Christ, while the Galatians have done so little for the kingdom of Jesus. However, this criticism needs to be tempered with the realization that this type of response to an adversary may have been customary in the culture at that time.

Paul degrades himself by giving in to name calling about those who upset the Philippians, referring to them as "dogs, evil-workers, mutilators of the flesh" (Ph 3:2). He engages in derisive comments about his opponents who urged the keeping of the dietary laws by saying, "Their God is their belly" (Ph 3:19). When his good news is in jeopardy of being misunderstood, he defends it with everything he has. This is true in Galatians 1:8-9 when he hurls anathema at those weak people who went back on what they had previously accepted to be true.[2]

In both the letters to the Galatians and Philippians, Paul fears that some of them were going to be unduly influenced by the Judaizers who viewed the observance of the Law as the basis for salvation. These Judaizers could cause divisions among the people. If people deviated from Paul's teachings, even in the slightest way, he became angry. There is an impression that there could be no exceptions to his teaching. It seems that whenever someone might harm his converts in any way, he becomes very anxious and rigid. In particular, he seems unmovable when it is a matter of forcing the observance of the Law on his converts. Because of these instances, people experienced him as an authoritarian leader.

When the Christians in Rome urge him not to go up to Jerusalem because they feared for his life, he refuses to be persuaded by their suggestions. His mind is made up that this is the will of God for him. In spite of the danger to his life and limb, he goes there anyway. Again, this confirms the impression that he was a rigid individual. The same conclusion can be reached when Barnabas urged him to accept Mark again as a companion on a future journey. Barnabas is not able to change Paul's mind. Paul is determined that Mark should not go on another missionary journey since he abandoned them previously. There are certain aspects of Paul's life where he is exceedingly firm and even rigid. Paul was a very zealous holy man who was also very human with his own less than perfect tendencies to be rigid, an authoritarian leader, and hostile in his expression of anger rather than open.

Conclusion

The Samaritan woman, the man born blind, and Peter are people who began the Lord's work with imperfect faith, yet Jesus called them to be his followers. At the time of their call, they believed in Jesus to the best of their ability. At the same time they were truly ministers of God's word, bringing people to Jesus as they shared their imperfect faith with others.

Peter and Paul deserve special mention as people who were

imperfect. Many times we official ministers place impossible expectations on ourselves. Since we are set aside for public ministry in the Church, we expect that we must be perfect. Since we are human beings, that is simply an unattainable goal. So we need to be comfortable as we place on ourselves only realistic expectations, allowing room for God's grace to work in achieving his goals.

If God writes straight with crooked lines, he can use the most unholy human beings to achieve his goals. Jesus chose the most ill-prepared men to be the foundation of his Church. The apostles were not educated men, they were not steeped in the Jewish Scriptures and traditions. They were not all of high moral character. Matthew was a tax collector and people in this profession were well known for their cheating, nor can we forget Judas who was described as a thief. They seemed intellectually slow at times because it took them so long to understand the spiritual nature of the kingdom. The apostles engaged in quarreling about who was the greatest among them immediately after Jesus predicted he was about to suffer and die.

Yet the Son of Man selected them after spending a night in prayer. His selection of these imperfect men turned out to have been a wise one, when we realize how Christianity spread from Jerusalem to the ends of the earth within a single generation after his ascension into heaven. Jesus' choice wasn't too bad when we consider that his Church has existed for almost two thousand years, guided today by other imperfect people.

Footnotes

[1] C.H. Dodd, *The Bulletin of John Ryland Library*, "The Mind of Paul," Vol. 17, January 1937, p. 93.

[2] Ernst Best, *Paul and His Converts* (The Sprunt Lectures), 1985, T.T. Part Edinburgh, E.H. 22LQ, 1988, pp. 118-120.